Daring to Feel

Daring to Feel

Violence, the News Media, and Their Emotions

Jody Santos

LEXINGTON BOOKS
A division of
ROWMAN & LITTLEFIELD PUBLISHERS, INC.
Lanham • Boulder • New York • Toronto • Plymouth, UK

Published by Lexington Books
A division of Rowman & Littlefield Publishers, Inc.
A wholly owned subsidiary of The Rowman & Littlefield Publishing Group, Inc.
4501 Forbes Boulevard, Suite 200, Lanham, Maryland 20706
www.lexingtonbooks.com

Estover Road, Plymouth PL6 7PY, United Kingdom

The author and publisher gratefully acknowledge permission for use of the
following sources:
Extracts from *Emotionally Involved: The Impact of Researching Rape* by Rebecca
Campbell, published in 2002 by Routledge, reprinted with permission.
Extracts from *Dangerous Lives: War and the Men and Women Who Report It* by
Anthony Feinstein, published in 2003 by Thomas Allen Publishers, reprinted
with permission.
The poems "Lens" and "Widow and Child" by Beth Murphy, reprinted with
permission.

British Library Cataloguing in Publication Information Available

Library of Congress Cataloging-in-Publication Data

The hardback edition of this book was previously catalogued by the Library of
Congress as follows:

Santos, Jody, 1966-
  Daring to feel : violence, the news media, and their emotions / Jody Santos.
      p. cm.
  Includes bibliographical references and index.
  1. Violence—Press coverage. 2. Violence in mass media. 3. Journalism—Objectivity.
4. Journalists—Mental health. 5. Journalism—Psychological aspects. I. Title.
  PN4784.V56S26 2009
  070.4'493036—dc22   2009034701

ISBN 978-0-7391-2529-8 (cloth : alk. paper)
ISBN 978-0-7391-2530-4(pbk. : alk. paper)
ISBN 978-0-7391-4401-5 (electronic)

For August

Contents

Acknowledgments   ix

Preface   xi

1 Stuck in Neutral: Violence and the News
   Media's Objective Mandate   1

2 Getting Engaged: The History of Emotional Reporting   15

3 From the Heart: The Benefits of Being Emotionally Invested   33

4 It's Personal: Gender, Medium, and More   47

5 Feeling the Pain: The Emotional Risks of Covering Violence   59

6 Road to Recovery: Finding New Ways to Talk
   About—and Heal from—Violence   71

Bibliography   83

Index   87

About the Author   91

Acknowledgments

This book has been so many years in the making that I have changed careers, had a child (my true labor of love), and moved twice since I first had the idea to explore the issue of emotions in journalism. I have many people to thank for giving me hope and confidence when I had neither and for letting me know that I was saying something when all I saw was a jumble of words on the page. Without their feedback and faith in my talents, I certainly would have given up long ago. They made me feel less alone in what, at times, was a very lonely process.

First, thanks to Deb Cohan, whose course on interpersonal violence at Northeastern University gave me the inspiration for this book. To Jim Ross and Alan Schroeder, two of my journalism professors at Northeastern, I owe a special thanks. They read very early drafts of this manuscript and never made me feel ashamed or embarrassed for tackling such a personal and taboo topic.

Of course, this book wouldn't exist without the people whose experiences I have chronicled. Thanks to Miles Moffeit, Hannah Allam, Daniel Vargas, Jim Willis, Bruce Shapiro, Laura Sullivan, Bruce Lundeen, David Handschuh, Kersti Yllo, and Beth Murphy in particular for daring to feel and for sharing their emotions with me. In addition, my sincere appreciation goes to Frank Ochberg, with whom I had several long conversations about the toll violence can take on those who cover it. Frank was so generous in sharing his knowledge with me. This book is stronger because of him.

To my colleagues at Assumption College, thank you for your friendship and belief in my work. I am particularly grateful to Ann Murphy and Mike Land, whom I trusted with some very rough drafts. Their insights and encouragement gave me the confidence to keep writing. I also would like to acknowledge members of my writing group, who took the time to try and understand what I was saying and improve upon it. And thank you so much, Lexington Books, for giving me a chance and publishing this manuscript!

My deepest appreciation goes to Rebecca Campbell, who was the first to suggest that I turn my idea into a book—and who provided support and encouragement at crucial moments. Rebecca has taught me the true meaning of the word "mentor." Her thoughts on thinking versus feeling live on in this book, and her constant faith in my work was, at times, my only lifeline. This book would not have happened without her. I am sure of it.

Finally, I owe a profound debt of gratitude to Meg Striepe for creating a safe place for me to explore my feelings and to my husband, David, for inspiring me to live life on a deeper, more emotional level. Over these last few years, I have relied on the love of so many, and in my vulnerability, they have helped me find my strength.

As I write this, my son is about to celebrate his second birthday. He has been walking for a while now and wants to explore life a little more each day. It's time for me to go after him—to stop talking about my emotions and really live them. And when the doubts come—as I know they will—I will remember the people in this book. They never stopped feeling even when it would have been easier for them to go numb. They acknowledged the pain and, as a result, were able to move past it. They will be in my heart, always.

Boston, Massachusetts
July 2009

Preface

While working as a magazine reporter fifteen years ago, I was assigned to write a story about a young man who'd murdered his estranged wife. His crime was particularly gruesome. Frank Moniz had stabbed twenty-five-year-old Maryellen more than fifty times with a nine-inch kitchen knife. It also was premeditated, as Frank had gone to her apartment to kill her once before, but had left after realizing her parents were there. Still, I sympathized with Frank in my article, questioning whether he "should be judged solely for the fifty knife strokes that killed Maryellen" or whether certain factors from his background—his debilitating epilepsy, for instance, or his father's physical abuse—should be taken into account. I described twenty-nine-year-old Frank as a "kid with epilepsy who spent most of his life stacking chairs and selling raffle tickets for the Catholic Youth Organization in his hometown." I did not go into Maryellen's background. I mentioned her only in reference to Frank—how she'd driven him to the hospital after a particularly bad seizure or how she'd tried to help him get a job.

Reading the article now, I see how it perpetuates certain myths about domestic violence. I portrayed Frank's crime as the result of his "tragic love" for Maryellen—he cared about her so much that he couldn't live without her. I gave no context for his actions, never referring to his crime as domestic abuse and barely mentioning the progression of his violence from stalking and threatening phone calls to murder. Instead, I framed Frank's crime as an unpredictable act committed by someone whom most had considered "harmless as a lamb."

At the time I wrote the article, I was twenty-six—perhaps too young to understand the dynamics of an abusive relationship or the violence involved in even non-physical acts like stalking. On another, more subconscious level, though, I did understand, as I had been stalked and threatened by an ex-boyfriend several years before. The police, his parents, and even my parents had not taken his actions seriously, instead treating him as a broken-hearted young man. They were more worried about his physical and emotional safety than mine.

When I set out to write the story of Frank and Maryellen, my own experiences did float back to me as vague memories from a distant time. But I was a journalist now, divorced from my past and emotions as a fulfillment of my mandate to be an objective observer. At the time, I did not make a real connection between Maryellen and myself. She was "other," her experiences as remote as a show I had watched on television. I relied on stereotypes of domestic abusers, believing those "truths" rather than my own. Frank loved Maryellen so much that he had to kill her. This is what I considered being objective.

Looking back on that experience, I don't blame myself for telling that story the way I did. In fact, I suspect that if I'd asked my editors, they, too, would have urged me to view my past experiences with caution, as possible contaminants to my work. But all these years later, I can't help but wonder what would have happened if I hadn't built that wall between Maryellen and myself, if I had recognized that our only real difference was that I had made it out of my situation alive. Stalked by my ex-boyfriend, I felt rage, hatred, helplessness, fear. If I had tapped into those emotions, perhaps I would have painted a more complex picture of domestic violence and its consequences.

As part of my research for this book, I interviewed a man who had been sexually abused by his parish priest and had filed a lawsuit against his abuser as an adult. The trial received a lot of publicity, and one of the reporters covering it confided in the victim that the priest had abused him as well. Thinking about that now, I struggle with whether the reporter should have taken the assignment. Clearly, he was biased and in danger of reliving his own trauma in listening to the details of the lawsuit. On the other hand, the reporter probably understood the consequences of the priest's actions on a level that only another survivor could. For the reporter, the barrier between us and them—journalists and subjects—did not exist with this story. He was free to see it in all its emotional complexity.

The way our feelings influence our thoughts and actions has long been a source of intense fascination among philosophers. Ever since Plato, intellectuals have made a clear distinction between thinking and feeling. The theory was that emotions sabotaged our ability to reason and that rational thought was far superior to empathy or intuition. But in the last two decades, philosophers and researchers alike have begun to make important connections between the heart and head. In 1995, internationally known psychologist Daniel Goleman argued that human intelligence had as much to do with emotion as it did with thought. In his bestseller *Emotional Intelligence: Why It Can Matter More Than IQ*, he maintains that we have "two brains, two minds"—the emotional and the rational—and that how well we do in life depends on our ability to "find the intelligent balance of the two."[1]

On the scientific side, these last twenty years have been marked by several major studies showing the interdependence of passion and reason. Armed with powerful brain-scanning technology, researchers have determined that emotions are the foundation of healthy thinking. In 2004, Harvard psychologist Joshua Greene showed how emotions played a role in resolving personal moral dilemmas. He discovered that whenever we consider harming another person, our brain generates a negative emotional response that discourages violence.[2]

In *Emotionally Involved: The Impact of Researching Rape*, psychologist Rebecca Campbell makes the case for the importance of emotions in her profession. She argues that, like journalists, social scientists have been taught to "devalue emotions as a source of knowledge."[3] But when Campbell and her research team interviewed more than a hundred rape survivors during a two-year study, they made some important discoveries about the importance of their feelings in the research process. They realized that the anger and fear they experienced talking with their subjects gave them powerful insights into sexual assault and its devastating impact. "Many of us on the research team began this work thinking about rape: rape was a concept to be operationally defined and debated," Campbell states in *Emotionally Involved*. "But, as the project continued, and the idea of rape was paired with the reality of names, faces, and tears, abstractness gave way to emotions. Feeling rape took over: an understanding based upon shared emotions—shock, betrayal, guilt, anger, hurt, and hope—with the rape victim."[4]

In trying to "define" rape from this more emotional perspective, Campbell writes:

> It is the debris, the skin, and the semen that is rubbed into you and all over you, again and again. It is spilled on you, dumped on you, and into you. It is the bacteria and the viruses that could be being mixed into you. It is the diseases, curable and incurable, that might be forced into you. Mixed into you, stirred into you—the semen into the blood, stirred by the force of a penis.
> That is what rape is.

Campbell explores the "affective component" of social science through the lens of rape because of its emotionally charged nature. She contends that rape "cannot truly be understood from a position of emotional neutrality, of academic 'objectivity,' because these problems are, at their core, emotional. They are, at their core, painful." More important, she says, researchers can't help but have feelings when repeatedly exposed to the pain of rape survivors.[5]

In a similar way, I chose to explore emotions among the American news media by interviewing journalists about the emotionally challenging topic of violence. By violence, I mean any physical act of aggression directed at another person or peoples—rape, murder, terrorism, family violence, battery, and war. I chose to explore the entire range of violence rather than focus on a subset (e.g., family violence) because the journalists I interviewed did not make distinctions among the type or scale of violence they covered. Those who allowed themselves to feel and get close to their subjects were just as likely to experience the pain of a rape survivor as they were of war refugees. No doubt, various factors—their family histories, the intensity and duration of the violence, the number of years they'd been immersed in the coverage—often intensified the journalists' experiences of violent events, but for them, there were no "degrees" to violence—no forms that were "worse" than others.

My interviewees came from a variety of backgrounds, their experiences ranging from documentary film production and television reporting to daily newspaper beats. Many had witnessed some of the worst tragedies in U.S. history. One photographer I interviewed barely survived the collapse of the World Trade Center, while a bureau chief for Knight Ridder saved her translator's life by spiriting her out of Iraq after the Iraqi woman's family was slain by insurgents. Following the Virginia Tech shootings, one reporter would close her eyes at night and think she heard the ringing cell phones in the pockets of the dead students. (Their parents had been trying to reach them on the day of the massacre to see if they were okay.) Another had sat at the hospital bedside of a woman who had been burned alive by her estranged husband.

My only real requirement for interviewing a journalist was that he or she had covered some form of violence. However, I did try to talk with a realistic representation of the news media. Of the twenty-two journalists I interviewed, half were women, and all but two of them were white—an unfortunate reflection of the lack of diversity in the newsroom. Sixteen of the journalists worked in print, while the other six worked in broadcast, either in radio or television. Some of the reporters I knew personally, while others I contacted after reading one of their stories and being moved by it. Every person with whom I spoke, whether I mention them here or not, helped shape my perspective on emotionally engaged reporting. My words are informed by their insights, my thoughts shaped by the long conversations I've had with them over these last few years.

In addition to talking with journalists, I reached out to psychiatrists and sociologists who have studied this concept of emotions in the social sciences and in other professions, and I reviewed dozens of studies examining how news coverage of violence impacts society's perception of the problem. In this way, I tried to follow my own advice, gathering scientific evidence to support my theories but also gaining a more qualitative perspective from the personal experiences of the journalists I interviewed.

While some of the reporters I contacted felt too uncomfortable to talk with me about their emotions, those who did were ready to acknowledge that the old model of emotional neutrality no longer worked for them—and perhaps never did. They dared to feel the pain of their stories and used that emotion to delve even deeper. Miles Moffeit, a reporter for the *Denver Post* who cowrote a groundbreaking series on rape in the military in 2004, compares his process to that of a method actor who "becomes" the person he or she is attempting to portray. If the actor doesn't feel the emotions of his or her character, the actor is not experiencing that character's "truth."

With his series, Moffeit wanted to feel his subjects' rage over what had happened to them—and over the military's attempts to cover up their assaults and allow their abusers to go free. "I wait for that reaction because I know it will come," he says. "If it doesn't come, I feel weird, like I don't get it yet. I don't get what these women have gone through."

Another reason I chose to explore reporters' emotions through the prism of violence is that it is one of the worst problems plaguing our nation today. Dozens of books have been published on how journalists' opinions and political leanings influence their work, but aren't some biases healthy, like a bias against people getting hurt? Shouldn't we be outraged when an average of three children die every day in this country from abuse or neglect,[6] when one out of three women will be abused by a partner at some point in her life,[7] when a staggering thirty-three people died at Virginia Tech in just the latest in a series of school massacres ravaging this country? And in telling our stories, shouldn't we oppose violence rather than compulsively tell both sides of the story? Why sanitize the brutality of war, for instance, by boiling it down to strategy? Why portray domestic violence as a single episode of he said/she said rather than the devastating epidemic that it is?

Frank Ochberg, a psychiatrist and pioneer in the fields of trauma and post-traumatic stress, says that as a society, we get "paradoxical pleasure" out of other people's pain and suffering. This is our way of coping with the terrible tragedies we hear and read about. In some ways, this coping process is like that of a child who indulges in fairy tales about scary monsters. The world is safe as long as those monsters are contained within a book. But while fairy tales may be a healthy way for children to deal with their emotions, most news stories about violent or tragic events rob victims of their dignity and fail to put those events in their proper context.

In an essay on why he became involved in the field of trauma, Ochberg explains why we all need to be concerned about violence:

> Our capacity for aggression allows us to organize ourselves and attain needed resources in ways that are historically and biologically human. But violence . . . is needlessly destructive aggression. Violence has never been adequately prevented and it threatens our existence. While we are not evolving into a more neurologically aggressive animal, we certainly are not overcoming our brutish heritage. And overcome it we must, because our impulse to hurt and harm affects so many more victims and potential victims as our weaponry grows more deadly and our deadly knowledge spreads.[8]

Journalists could help overcome this heritage by taking a stand against violence. While this would mean straying from the old journalistic model of detachment, the news media ultimately would be taking a higher ethical road in attempting to put a stop to this deadly force.

THE SUBJECTIVE JOURNALIST

When the news media have strayed from the mandate of neutrality in their coverage of violence, their reports have had an impact, both on the issues they've covered and on the profession itself. During the Vietnam War, as the news media became increasingly savvy to the government's lies at home and abroad, early correspondents such as Michael Herr abandoned journalism's normally distant stance for something more personal. "Conventional journalism could no more reveal this war than conventional firepower could win it," Herr wrote after visiting Vietnam in 1967.[9] Reporting for *Esquire* magazine, Herr knew he needed to describe what it actually felt like to be fighting a war because its horrors were so beyond his American audience's comprehension. When his article became a book in 1977, he began it in the first person. His prose took on the paranoid, disoriented tone of the troops with whom he lived:

> Whenever I heard something outside of our clenched little circle I'd practically flip, hoping to God that I wasn't the only one who'd noticed it. A couple of rounds fired off in the dark a kilometer away and the Elephant would be there kneeling on my chest. . . . Once I thought I saw a light moving in the jungle and I caught myself just under a whisper saying, "I'm not ready for this, I'm not ready for this."[10]

In a kind of post-traumatic stress usually associated with soldiers, Herr internalized the atrocities he'd witnessed. He made no pretense of objectivity.

Herr's blunt observations about the war—and those of other writers such as David Halberstam and Norman Mailer—helped change the dialogue around Vietnam. With the normally objective press taking a stand, a kind of moral urgency emerged that hadn't existed before, fueling the antiwar movement. A more recent example of emotionally engaged reporting is CNN reporter Anderson Cooper's coverage of Hurricane Katrina in 2005. As the extent of the disaster dawned on him, Cooper interviewed Senator Mary Landrieu, a Democrat from Louisiana, about the government's woeful response. But rather than criticize her colleagues, Landrieu blithely thanked them for all of their hard work and support. His voice shaking with anger, Cooper lashed out at her:

> I've got to tell you, there are a lot of people here who are very upset, and very angry, and very frustrated. And when they hear politicians slap—you know, thanking one another, it just, you know, it kind of cuts them the wrong way right now, because literally there was a body on the streets of this town yesterday being eaten by rats because this woman had been lying in the street for forty-eight hours. And there's not enough facilities to take her up. Do you get the anger that is out here?[11]

After Cooper's interview, bloggers lit up the Internet, cheering on the CNN reporter. Although some critics said he went too far in embarrassing a public official on live television, others applauded Cooper's ire as a sign that someone finally had cared enough to speak out. And the CNN reporter's outburst did seem to have an impact, at least on Landrieu. When the senator was interviewed by another network a few days later, she was much more critical of the government's actions. On *ABC News*, she threatened to "punch" President Bush and chastised his administration for failing to grasp the "magnitude of this disaster."[12]

In his bestselling memoir, *Dispatches From the Edge: A Memoir of War, Disasters, and Survival*, Cooper explains the reason behind his outburst: The situation was simply too dire to mitigate with objective language. "In normal times you can't always say what's right and what's wrong. The truth is not always clear. Here, however, all the doubt is stripped away," he writes, referring to those regions impacted by Hurricane Katrina. "This isn't about Republicans and Democrats, theories and politics. Relief is either here or it's not. Corpses don't lie."[13]

In revealing his emotions on national television, Cooper defied a trend that has been part of the journalistic tradition for more than a century. Indeed, the objective model is still taught in most journalism schools, even though we all know that absolute objectivity is impossible. It remains a central tenet of the journalistic faith because we have yet to come up with another way to define ourselves. But in holding up this impossible ideal as the industry standard, we automatically set ourselves up for failure. Despite all of our recent attempts to institutionalize objectivity with various codes of ethics and disciplinary procedures, our audiences have never trusted us less, and media bias is one of the main reasons why.[14] What's more, the enormous popularity of Web blogs shows the increasing popularity of writing that's more from the heart or gut, more subjective than objective in nature.

In pointing out the flaws of the objective model, I am not suggesting that we all should start pontificating on issues like the effects of violence. This is not a call for advocacy journalism—or for "opinion journalism" practiced by the likes of Bill O'Reilly. (In chapter 2, I will address the danger of passionate reporting slipping into political advocacy.) I am also not suggesting that in delving into our emotions, we should abandon our professional standards and not carefully gather the whos, whats, wheres, and whens of our stories. I don't want to confuse objectivity with reality—to suggest that nothing is real so why bother searching for truth. If anything, I believe we need to do even more research, to assemble even more facts, before we truly can begin to grasp how we feel about something.

What I am saying, though, is that in pursuing objectivity above all else, we could be having a negative impact on our stories—and on our audience's perceptions of us. Rather than engendering trust and helping us see the whole of a situation, the objective model could be having the reverse effect. By placing more value on thoughts over emotions, our heads over our hearts, we are essentially straightjacketing ourselves and operating at only half our capacities. As journalists, we know what we know because of who we are. In trying to silence parts of ourselves in our stories, then, are we not filing incomplete, and perhaps even inaccurate, stories because we do not "know" them as well as we could? Why not treat the subjective as a legitimate source of knowledge? After all, what could be fairer to our subjects than using every resource we have—our thoughts, feelings, sensory perceptions, memories, histories, and so forth—in reporting our stories?

ON THE EMOTIONAL BRINK

As journalists, we have reached a critical point in expressing our feelings. "We've been battered so emotionally over the last seven years," David Handschuh, a staff photographer for the *New York Daily News*, tells me. "We've been plastered with mega-level tragedies, from Katrina and nine/eleven to the tsunami and Iraq War." These catastrophes have pushed us to the emotional brink, and now cracks are starting to appear in our objective facade. Dubbed the "emo-anchor," Cooper and his outburst on CNN seemed to give other reporters permission to reveal their feelings about Katrina, with some shedding tears or openly seething with anger on the air. Many within the industry applauded this apparent shift among the American media. On *Fox News Watch*, *Newsday* columnist Jim Pinkerton said that while some of the journalists covering the storm "clearly lost some of their objectivity" in becoming emotionally involved in the story, they "gained some of their humanity."[15] And on CNN's *Showbiz Tonight*, Jeff Alan, author of *Anchoring America*, told host A. J. Hammer that Katrina journalists "all of a sudden . . . weren't prepackaged reporters anymore. They were human beings with a microphone."[16]

Bruce Shapiro, executive director of the Dart Center for Journalism & Trauma, a New York-based global resource center for journalists who cover violence, says the images of Katrina—the bodies floating in the canal, the people trapped in the convention center—evoked a kind of journalism that Americans hadn't seen in centuries. He calls it a "journalism of outrage." The stories from the storm "sprang from journalists' deep sense of injustice," he tells me, and since Katrina, the U.S. news media have taken more of an aggressive role in their reporting. "There has been an uptick in the amount and quality of investigative journalism," Shapiro contends, "and I think there is more of a sense again that journalism can make a difference and change the world."

Handschuh sees Katrina as one of several key moments in the news media's gradual awakening to their feelings. "Personally, Columbine was the light bulb for me," he says. "For many people who went over there it was very, very important." A veteran photographer, Handschuh had covered other tragedies like the bombing of Pan Am Flight 103 over Lockerbie, Scotland, but Columbine was his first school shooting. Handschuh, a father of three, was overcome with emotion at the scene. "I cried at Columbine," he says, "and so did a lot of other people." Handschuh and the other photographers and reporters at Columbine gradually opened up to one another—and started a dialogue. "It was journalists talking to other journalists about how they felt," he says. "It was a kind of collective growing of the news media."

After September 11, Handschuh contends, this dialogue only intensified because so many journalists were personally affected by the story. Handschuh himself nearly lost his life as he chronicled the horror raining down on him at the World Trade Center. When the South Tower had begun to crumble, the photographer had been swept up by what he would later describe as "a tornado of night." "It was like getting hit in the back by a wave at the beach. Instead of salt water, this wave was made of hot gravel and glass, cement and metal," Handschuh wrote in an essay titled

"A Lens on Life and Death." The *Daily News* staffer had landed under a vehicle; he was trapped by debris and certain he would die: "I reached for my cell phone to call home and tell everyone that I loved them, but it was gone. My pager was gone. My glasses were gone."[17]

Handschuh eventually was rescued by firefighters and had major surgery on his leg. He took a year to recover from both his physical and emotional injuries, seeking counseling to deal with his post-traumatic stress. When he returned to work, he told his editors he never wanted to photograph someone who was dead or dying again. To this day, he has not shown anyone some of the more gruesome images he shot on September 11. "Nine/eleven sent up a flare in the community that we are affected by the stories we cover and that we should no longer have a 'just suck it up' mentality," he says.

Of course, there are risks for those reporters who become emotionally involved in their stories. "[W]hen passions surge the balance tips: it is the emotional mind that captures the upper hand, swamping the rational mind," Goleman contends in *Emotional Intelligence*.[18] After September 11, a patriotic fervor swept across the news media, with national broadcasts sporting red, white, and blue graphics and some reporters wearing American flag pins on their lapels. On the *Late Show with David Letterman*, even CBS icon Dan Rather pledged his allegiance to the U.S., vowing to do whatever the president asked of him. "George Bush is the president. He makes the decisions, and you know, as just one American, wherever he wants me to line up, just tell me where," Rather told Letterman.[19]

In hindsight, it's safe to say that journalists' emotions—their patriotism and fear, anger and grief—did blind them to certain realities about Bush's rush to war and kept them from asking important questions. To be fair, though, the news media constantly battle a kind of Catch-22. When they don't express emotion, they're accused of being heartless exploitation artists; when they do, they're criticized for not being vigorous enough in their reporting or for faking emotions to boost ratings. Even the journalists covering Katrina did not completely escape such criticism. In an article for the Dart Center, BBC News correspondent Gavin Hewitt wrote that tears on screen "make the correspondent the eye of the story rather than the people who are actually suffering." And *USA Today* contributor Harriet Rubin called the Katrina coverage "dangerous and irresponsible." "Reporters' salty tears went down, over the air, a little funky, like MSG," she wrote, "as they puzzled over how best to milk more flood victim grief and find the silver lining—a few poignant family photos, a sense of closure upon returning to find a house completely gone."[20]

With all these mixed signals, the press seemed to emerge from 9/11 and Katrina so hypersensitive to criticism that when the next national tragedy struck, their coverage, at least on the national level, took on the remote, wooden tones of those careful not to offend. In April 2007, a young man named Seung-Hui Cho shot thirty-two innocent people and then himself at Virginia Tech in Blacksburg, Virginia. As if on cue, the news media swarmed the campus and began asking the usual questions. Dealing with a population that clearly had been traumatized, many of the reporters seemed to be in shock as well. Accused of going too far in the past with overly aggressive reporting or overly emotional accounts, the news media this time often delved no deeper than asking what witnesses had seen or heard. They also seemed to distance themselves from the massacre with bland, neutral language, referring to Cho as the "shooter" or "gunman." Perhaps most troubling, they offered simplistic explanations (Cho played violent video games, for instance, or had been bullied by high school classmates) for a complex problem—the epidemic of school shootings plaguing this nation.

Looking back, I wonder if I distanced myself from the story of Frank and Maryellen Moniz because I couldn't face my own pain and humiliation over what had happened to me. Instead, I hid behind the mask of objectivity—and completely disconnected from my personal story. I remember the time I interviewed Frank in prison. He was sitting across from me in his state-issued jumpsuit, and his attorney was on my right. Suddenly, a cockroach scuttled across the floor, and Frank squashed it with the tip of his shoe. "Hey, have some respect for life!" his attorney said. At first, I didn't get the joke—or maybe I was too stunned for it to sink in. But as the enormity of the attorney's twisted humor finally dawned on me, I just sat there, awkwardly grinning and shaking my head. Even now, all these years later, I am struck by just how far removed I was from my own inner workings—not just from my emotions but from my sense of justice and the sacredness of life.

What I didn't realize then, but clearly see now, is that my values and emotions were creeping out in other ways, in other stories. Miles Moffeit, who co-wrote the series on rape in the military for the *Denver Post*, once told me, "A childhood of adversity leads to an impulse to attack adversity as an adult." I think about this a lot now in terms of my own reporting. In the years following the Moniz article, I covered dozens of other stories involving interpersonal violence, from clergy abuse and domestic assault to gang murders and date rape. Taking inventory of these stories now, I wonder whether I was really running away from my past or running toward it. In his book, Cooper, whose brother committed suicide while Anderson was still in college, talks about how that personal tragedy fueled his professional desire to cover wars and other emotionally intense situations. "I wanted to be someplace where emotions were palpable, where the pain outside matched the pain I was feeling inside," he wrote in *Dispatches from the Edge*. "I needed balance, equilibrium, or as close to it as I could get."[21]

When I started out in journalism, I suppose I was in search of a similar emotional outlet. I feel a certain amount of guilt in saying that now, as if I'd been trying to take something that didn't quite belong to me. Rather than telling my own story and laying myself bare, I was stealing other people's stories, almost as a form of self-medication. Years after I wrote about Frank and Maryellen Moniz, I became a world traveler of sorts, working as an alternative press editor, television producer, and documentary filmmaker. Along the way, I met dozens of women with stories like Maryellen's—women who had fled abusive husbands and were now homeless, who'd been stalked by ex-lovers or stuck in abusive relationships. But in all that time, I never once cried about a story I covered. On some level this bothered me, even though I told myself I was better off not getting too emotionally involved.

The event that I see as my turning point, my Columbine or September 11, happened about eight years ago. At the time, I was producing and directing a public television documentary about the trafficking of young girls in Nepal, and my crew and I had gone to visit a safehouse for girls who'd been liberated from prostitution. At first, the headmistress would not allow me to interview any of her young wards, but after we politely endured her three-hour interview and tour, she relented and led us into a small room. Eventually, a girl of about fourteen appeared in the doorway. She was disfigured, with one leg shorter than the other, and abnormally small for her age. Her thick, dark hair was pulled back in a ponytail, and she shuffled under the weight of her oversized shawl. At age eleven, she had been forced into an arranged marriage. Her mother-in-law later sold her into prostitution because the girl's family hadn't been able to afford a dowry.

As my subject took a seat opposite from me, I smiled at her but really didn't know what to do or say. I somehow wanted to connect with her, but I didn't speak Nepalese. More important, what did I, a pampered American, possibly have in common with my interviewee? Wondering how I could bridge the gap between us, I reached into my backpack for some small token I could present to her. All I found was a stick of Wrigley's Doublemint Gum, but when I offered it to her, she gratefully accepted. That simple gesture seemed to break the spell between us, and through a translator, she went on to tell me her story. I can't say I was moved at that particular moment, but later that afternoon, my cameraperson told me something that finally brought me back to myself. After she'd taken the gum from me, the girl had retrieved a pen and scrawled her initials on the wrapper. Then she'd quickly put the gum in her pocket so that no one else would see it. She had wanted to hold on to this one small thing. No one would take it away from her.

That night, back at my hotel room in Katmandu, I cried about a story for the first time, my pillow wet with my tears. I wish I could say that I felt relieved, but instead I felt fear and a sense of betrayal. By allowing myself to feel, I was holding up a mirror to the rest of the profession, challenging the notion of objective reporting as the moral high ground. No wonder I have not written about this experience until now.

When I returned from Nepal, I continued to produce documentaries for another two years. It is only in hindsight that I see how my experience there began to change the way I viewed my work. I was tired of making a living off other people's misery. I was tired of standing on the outside, feeling superior to those of whom I spoke. I was also physically and mentally spent, possibly from having to hold so much back. At the age of thirty-eight, I decided to go to graduate school, earn my degree, and teach journalism. I wanted to make sure that the next generation of reporters didn't repeat my mistakes. I wanted them to dig in to their instincts and to trust what they saw and felt.

The funny thing is, your experiences have a way of following you. During my first semester of graduate school, I signed up for a sociology course on interpersonal violence, and that's when I began to connect the dots of my life. As I immersed myself in the assigned readings, memories of my ex-boyfriend broke the surface of my thoughts, and I saw how his violence had started long before the stalking incident, how his words and actions had menaced me almost since the day I'd first met him at age sixteen. I also saw how susceptible I had been to this type of dynamic. Growing up in a strict Catholic family that had stressed obedience over individuality, I'd never been allowed to assert myself. Again and again, I'd bowed to someone else's will, and when I finally had stood up to intimidation with my ex-boyfriend, he had threatened my life. Essentially, I'd faced the possibility of extinction, only because I had found my voice and had wanted to use it. Whether I was conscious of it or not, the blatant injustice of this fueled my desire to become a journalist. Being a reporter gave me a certain kind of power I'd never had before, a way to control the ending of a story, to dole out or withhold judgment as I saw fit, to rescue people and possibly even myself.

This book grew out of a project for that class on interpersonal violence. After reading Campbell's *Emotionally Involved*, I started interviewing fellow journalists about their feelings about violence. On the day I presented my findings to the class, I broke down while talking about a journalist who'd written a story about a woman whose estranged husband had set her on fire. In a sense, I was proving the very theory I'd been testing out—that we can't help but be moved when exposed to the painful stories of others. My tears were as awkward for me as I'm sure they were for my classmates, but in that moment, I crossed a line. What had long been in my heart finally made it to my head. I would never view my role as a journalist the same way again.

The idea for this book sat for two more years before I finally decided to do something with it. After plunging so deeply into my emotions, perhaps I simply needed to step back for a while, to achieve what Campbell describes as a kind of "emotional peace" around my topic. The decision about whether to proceed with this book—and to reveal my own feelings and past experiences—was a difficult one. But ultimately I decided that my emotions did more harm than good when locked inside of me. Most of the journalists I interviewed felt the same way.

My goal for this project is to move beyond the third person in journalism to the first, because the word "I" has been banished from the news media's lexicon for too long. In order to redefine ourselves beyond the objective model—and to reclaim our audiences and their trust in the process—we must turn inward and examine ourselves as the primary sources of our work. In her book, Campbell refers to this process as "researching the researcher."[22] For my purposes, I am reporting on the reporter.

NOTES

1. Daniel Goleman, *Emotional Intelligence: Why It Can Matter More than IQ* (New York: Bantam Books, 1995), 28, 29.

2. Joshua D. Greene et al., "The Neural Bases of Cognitive Conflict and Control in Moral Judgment," *Neuron* 44 (October 14, 2004): 389–400.

3. Rebecca Campbell, *Emotionally Involved: The Impact of Researching Rape* (New York: Routledge, 2002), 15.

4. Campbell, *Emotionally Involved*, 9–10.

5. Campbell, *Emotionally Involved*, 9, 115, 117.

6. Ching-Tung Lung and Deborah Daro, "Current Trends in Child Abuse Reporting and Fatalities: The Results of the 1995 Annual Fifty State Survey," Chicago: National Committee to Prevent Child Abuse (1996).

7. Karen Scott Collins et al., "Health Concerns Across a Woman's Lifespan: The Commonwealth Fund 1998 Survey of Women's Health," The Commonwealth Fund (1999).

8. Frank Ochberg, "There Is Reason in Action," in *Mapping Trauma and Its Wake: Autobiographic Essays by Pioneer Trauma Scholars* (Routledge Psychosocial Stress Series, 31), ed. Charles R. Figley (New York: Routledge, 2005), 137.

9. Marc Weingarten, *The Gang That Wouldn't Write Straight: Wolfe, Thompson, Didion, and the New Journalism Revolution* (New York: Crown Publishers, 2006), 163.

10. Michael Herr, *Dispatches* (New York: Vintage Books, 1991), 4–5.

11. Anderson Cooper, *Dispatches from the Edge: A Memoir of War, Disasters, and Survival* (New York: HarperCollins, 2006), 143–144.

12. Mary Landrieu, Interview with George Stephanopoulos, *This Week with George Stephanopoulos*, ABC News, September 4, 2005.

13. Cooper, *Dispatches*, 141.

14. Project for Excellence in Journalism, *State of the News Media 2007: An Annual Report on American Journalism*, 2007.

15. Jim Pinkerton, Interview with Eric Burns, *Fox News Watch*, Fox News Network, September 10, 2005.

16. Jeff Alan, Interview with A. J. Hammer, *Showbiz Tonight*, CNN, September 12, 2005.

17. David Handschuh, "A Lens on Life and Death," PoynterOnline January 8, 2002, www.poynter.org/content/content_view.asp?id=4673 (accessed September 8, 2006).

18. Goleman, *Emotional Intelligence*, 9.

19. Dan Rather, Interview with David Letterman, *Late Show with David Letterman*, CBS, September 17, 2001.

20. Harriet Rubin, "TV: Why a little 'dry' journalism would serve us all," *USA Today*, September 29, 2005, 13(A).

21. Cooper, *Dispatches*, 46.

22. Campbell, *Emotionally Involved*, 9.

1

✒

Stuck in Neutral

Violence and the News Media's Objective Mandate

Two and a half weeks after the Oklahoma City bombing in 1995, Jim Willis and a dozen other journalists were stationed atop the rubble pile that used to be the Alfred P. Murrah Federal Building. Survivors of the explosion, their families, and friends were holding an impromptu memorial service, and Willis, a veteran reporter and editor who'd grown up in Oklahoma, was covering it for a local daily. A cameraperson from Reuters had fastened a rose to his tripod. Willis had pinned a ribbon to his lapel for the same purpose—as a kind of personal remembrance for the innocent people who had lost their lives in the bombing. After the ceremony, a group of younger reporters challenged Willis's small display of empathy. "We feel it's like taking sides," they told him. Of course, this wasn't Willis's intention, but he still was startled by their reaction to his ribbon. Could there really be sides to such a brutal crime, he wondered. Could anyone sympathize with someone who'd blown up 168 people, 19 of them children?

Even though most reporters agree that "pure" objectivity is unattainable, the vast majority of us still believe it is a goal worth striving for, even (or perhaps I should say, particularly) at the scene of such heinous crimes as the Oklahoma City bombing. The mandate of objectivity gives us a clear, single purpose—to gather the facts. It allows us to put aside our own feelings about the tragic events we cover and see the world "as it is," thus ensuring fairness, accuracy, and truth in our stories.

Modeled after scientific knowing, journalistic objectivity involves a systematic approach to covering news. To claim impartiality, the news media adhere to certain rituals in their writing and reporting. These include obtaining "both sides" of every story, keeping a healthy distance from our

1

subjects to avoid any conflicts of interest, relying on official sources like the police for unbiased accounts, and putting quotes around any opinions expressed in our stories to make it clear that we are not taking sides.[1] Without these rules, the thinking goes, the news media would slide into what one author describes as a "journalistic Woodstock, where everything except disciplined reporting is considered cool."[2] Objectivity, or impartiality, separates us from the blatantly opinionated Bill O'Reillys of the world. If we succumb to subjectivity, the fear is that society would lose its last real arbiters of truth. Who would be left to sort out facts from politics, reality from spin control, and good intentions from bad ones? Without objectivity, readers and viewers would bob in a sea of opinionated blogs and amateur speculation. A separate identifiable truth would cease to exist.

This ideal of objectivity is first introduced in journalism school, both at the undergraduate and graduate levels. It seems like every journalism textbook has the requisite case study of the pro-life reporter who should keep his or her opinions to him or herself and should never be allowed to cover the abortion debate—or the small-town journalist who loses his or her job for displaying a bumper sticker in support of a local candidate. Student journalists are taught to embrace a kind of civic celibacy and to stay away from those stories about which they have strong personal feelings. They learn to write in the third person and stick to the whos, whats, wheres, whens, and hows of journalism.

On a professional level, the majority of journalists seem to take a perverse pride in being able to remain detached, more like cops than civilians in their attitudes toward crime and violence. Unlike in other professions, many of us consider it an asset if we can wall off our personal thoughts and feelings. Lawyers are allowed to be passionate advocates for their clients, and judges and juries, upon hearing all the evidence, are expected to form an opinion and issue a verdict. The legal system works according to this subjective principle. Even doctors are allowed to take a patient's "side" in terms of his or her care—to unequivocally advocate for what's best for that patient.

But although we work in the real world and not in a laboratory, journalists are expected to neutralize and segregate their subjectivities as counter to the reporting process. Essentially, we have learned to become what sociologist Susan Krieger calls "invisible authors" of our work.[3] We rarely are allowed to acknowledge the self in our stories, even though the stories would not exist without us. While we all admit that we can never be completely objective, we are not allowed to draw too much attention to this fact in our writing. Instead, we use what Krieger describes in her field as "standard terms and depersonalized voices that camouflage the self."[4] On TV, we read the news in detached, professional voices, and we package news on the Web in disembodied snippets, often without even a byline or any other acknowledgment of our presence. We hide behind the official language of journalism—the "no comments" and "allegedlies"—rather than reveal any part of ourselves.

Sometimes our denials of our subjectivities are so extreme, they border on the absurd. Asked whether the Pentagon was a legitimate target for the terrorists of September 11, ABC News President David Westin once told a roomful of Columbia Journalism School students that objectivity required him to have no opinion on the matter. His statement, made not long after the attacks, prompted a flurry of embarrassing press coverage for him. People wondered how anyone living in the U.S., let alone the president of a top network's news division, could not have an opinion about one of the worst tragedies in our nation's history.[5]

OBJECTIVITY AND VIOLENCE

The news media's obsession with objectivity can be particularly problematic when it comes to stories about violence. By blindly obeying the journalistic mandate to remain neutral, we often fail to absorb the tragic proportions of a violent event. We can become immune to the suffering of others, which often *is* the story when it comes to violence. Even worse, the objective mandate can lead us to conclude that viewing suffering or abuse dispassionately, or even cynically, is more morally correct than viewing it with outrage or compassion.

While cynicism may be part of our attempts to keep our emotional distance at emotionally trying times, Minnesota public radio reporter Dan Gunderson maintains that it can warp our stories more than any other human feeling. "Looking at a story with cynicism, making jokes about people who have been hurt, is looking at it through another lens. It's not understanding the story," he says. "I've said to myself many times, 'Put the cynicism away and feel this,' because I know that if I don't, I'll get so disconnected, I won't be able to do a story justice."

There are other problems with the news media's objective approach to violence as well. In our compulsion to "get both sides of the story," we often downplay the severity of a crime and infer that victims of school shootings, terrorist attacks, and domestic abuse are somehow to blame for what happened to them. In addition, our reliance on police as the main sources of information about crimes often reinforces certain stereotypes about violence that may be harmful to survivors. And, finally, by sticking to the whos, whats, wheres, whens, and hows of journalism and rarely asking why a violent crime has occurred, we portray violence as an out-of-the-blue, unavoidable occurrence rather than as part of a larger social problem.

Most of the research on media coverage of violence focuses on stories about the abuse of women. This research often takes a feminist approach, meaning it examines how public depictions of gender violence reinforce the very inequalities that encourage men to abuse women in the first place. As Drew Humphries notes in *Women, Violence, and the Media: Readings in Feminist Criminology*, a key feminist principle is that "'systems of knowledge' reflect masculine understandings of the world and that these systems legitimate the 'natural authority' of men and the subordination of women." In all forms of media, Humphries contends, "masculine assumptions about women's experience with violence are remarkably persistent."[6] Some of these assumptions are that female victims play a role in their abuse (they should have been more careful, they engaged in immoral behavior, or somehow provoked their attackers) and that the perpetrators are not completely to blame for their actions—they were mentally ill or heartbroken over a recent breakup.

Several years ago Cathy Ferrand Bullock and Jason Cubert, then graduate research assistants at the University of Washington, examined the news coverage of domestic violence fatalities over the course of a year in Washington State. Their study encompassed the coverage of 44 cases in 40 newspapers, making for a total of 230 articles. What they found was that almost *half* the stories offered some kind of excuse for the perpetrator—he or she had mental health problems, for instance, or had abused alcohol or grown up in an abusive home. Even worse, almost 20 percent of the articles, by nature of the reporting and the quotes used, suggested the victim was to blame for the abuse. These stories "seemed to indicate that women maintained and almost sought out relationships with abusers," the study's authors contend. "For example, in one article, a victim's ex-sister-in-law noted that 'Ronnie had a habit of getting with men that abused her.'"[7]

Daniel Vargas, a former *Houston Chronicle* reporter, has witnessed such victim-blaming firsthand. He once wrote a series about a woman who had been set on fire by her estranged husband, and he recalls how one of his editors suggested he explore the husband's motive for the crime. "An editor brought into question the paternity of one of the children," says Vargas. "I told them that we couldn't get caught up in those things, that there was no gray area here. There are no legitimate reasons for setting a woman on fire."

In her book *News Coverage of Violence Against Women: Engendering Blame*, media analyst Marian Meyers says that when it comes to gender violence, there are not always two sides to every story. "Journalists, who have been socialized to unquestioningly seek objectivity through balance, must recognize that, in most cases, anti-woman violence cannot be balanced," she says. "Attempting to do so denies the seriousness of violence against women and raises questions about the woman's behavior in provoking the attack."[8]

In covering violence, the news media can fall into other types of bias traps as well. As I've already mentioned, we tend to rely on police officers as our main sources of information, presumably because they will provide an unbiased account of an incident. But Ferrand Bullock and Cubert, authors of the University of Washington study, challenge this assumption. In the articles they reviewed, the police tended to "dehumanize the crime" by focusing more on the mechanics of it than the people involved and the dynamics of their relationship. What's more, the police did not characterize the fatalities as a culmination of events between the abuser and victim or as part of a larger social problem. Instead, they portrayed the violence as isolated incidents to which they, the police, had appropriately responded.[9]

In this way, feminist researchers argue, police officers—and the journalists who rely on them—ultimately serve the needs of patriarchy by not acknowledging the dominant role gender bias plays in the abuse of women. "By presenting stories of violence against women as separate, discreet incidents, the news . . . reinforces the idea that this violence is a matter of isolated pathology or deviance, related only to the particular circumstances of those involved and unconnected to the larger structure of patriarchal domination and control," says Meyers. "This mirage of individual pathology denies the social roots of violence against women and relieves the larger society of any obligation to end it."[10]

Another reason why gender abuse is not often reported in a larger social context is that our news tends to be facts-based rather than analytical in nature. As noted journalism educator James Carey explains:

> The first injunction of journalists is to stay with the facts; facts provide the elements of the story. But causes, consequences, and motives are not themselves facts. Because journalists are above all else empiricists, the why must elude them.[11]

In covering violence, the news media often will describe how a crime played out and who committed it—the who, what, where, when, and how of a story—but rarely will we delve into the larger question of why except on a superficial level. Our answers to why tend to focus more on individual motives than on underlying social problems. Carey identifies this "over-reliance on motive explanations" as a "pervasive weakness" among the American news media. "Motive explanations are too easy," he says. "It takes time, effort, and substantial knowledge to find a cause, whereas motives are available for a phone call."[12]

Motive explanations also reinforce society's tendency to view domestic violence through an individual frame rather than a cultural one. The result, according to Nancy Berns, author of *Framing the Victim: Domestic*

Violence, Media, and Social Problems, is public policy that focuses more on individual solutions—e.g., counseling—than societal ones, such as changing public attitudes about violence against women. "Why are people not asking about why individuals abuse others? Why do they not ask how abusers continue to get away with their behavior?" asks Berns. "Why are so few people talking about violence itself or social and cultural factors that foster it? Why are most media stories about victims?"[13]

Overall, Meyers maintains that no matter how much the news media wave the flag of objectivity, we are hopelessly biased in our coverage of violence, particularly in our choices of which crimes we report. Because we do not have any clear guidelines to help us define a story's newsworthiness, we tend to rely on our own judgment or gut response in picking our assignments. Not surprisingly, then, we tend to write about crimes involving people like ourselves—crimes that reflect our own interests and biases.

To prove her theory, Meyers conducted in-depth interviews with nine journalists in Atlanta—five women and four men. All of them were white and had covered the murder of a local white woman. Tragically, the woman had been shot in the head in front of her two young sons, and her husband, a prominent judge and attorney, had been charged with hiring the gunman who'd killed her. "Given the relatively large number of murders and acts of violence to cover in Atlanta, one might well ask why some crimes of violence are covered and others are not," Meyers says. When asked, the reporters said newsworthiness was hard to define but that the crime had to be "unusual" or have a "gee whiz" quality to it. They said they knew a good story when they saw one—that their "news instinct" told them so.

For Meyers, this is a clear indication of bias, with reporters defining what was newsworthy and unusual. She states:

> Reporters' inability to define news as other than an instinct, as something that would elicit a "gee whiz," allows them to make collectively subjective decisions based on consensual notions of what is newsworthy. That consensus, although appearing to be based on common sense and what is "natural" (as in, it is natural that the public should be interested in "high society and big money"), reflects the dominant ideology in its underlying assumptions and values.

Meyers notes that the nine white journalists she interviewed represented the predominantly white perspective of the mainstream media—and the dominant voice of our patriarchal society. As a result, she concludes, the choices they made ultimately served "the biases—and interests—of a patriarchal society."[14]

Sociologists Michelle Meloy and Susan Miller also explored the issue of the news media's bias in our coverage of violence when they examined two eerily similar cases, one of which received much more press attention than the other. In the first, twenty-seven-year-old Laci Peterson had been eight months pregnant when she disappeared on Christmas Eve 2002. The recovery of her body (and, later, of the remains of her eight-month-old baby) in San Francisco Bay made national headlines, and her husband Scott's subsequent murder trial sparked a media frenzy. Laci was a stay-at-home wife whom the press characterized as the girl next door. She "epitomized traditional notions of what women should do with their lives," say Meloy and Miller, and as a result, the news media deemed her story newsworthy.

The second case involved the 2002 disappearance of twenty-four-year-old Evelyn Hernandez and her five-year-old son, Alex. Hernandez also had been pregnant at the time she went missing, and her remains also were found floating in San Francisco Bay. (Her son's body was never recovered.) What's more, Hernandez's boyfriend, the father of the unborn child, also was a suspect in the case. But despite the similarities to the Peterson case, the media did not pay nearly as much attention to the deaths of Hernandez, her son, and unborn child. When they did write about them, they tended to focus on Hernandez's single motherhood and out-of-wedlock pregnancy. Hernandez apparently was less of a "legitimate" victim than Peterson,[15] Meloy and Miller conclude, so the news media considered her murder less worthy of attention.

Put simply, says Meyers, "news coverage of violent crimes reveals society's biases and prejudices. It tells us who is valued and who is not; whose life has meaning and whose life is insignificant; who has power and who does not."[16]

By focusing on "the facts" and relying on official sources like police, journalists are committing a kind of professional negligence when it comes to portrayals of violence. We are presenting the public with a distorted view of the problem—one that presents violence as unpredictable and, thus, unstoppable. In addition, we are clearly biased in terms of which violent crimes we choose to cover, inherently implying that some lives are more valuable than others. As I will discuss in the next section, the news media, as interpreters of reality, play a vital role in how society views—and ultimately responds to—the problem of violence. Our accounts count. As a result, we need to rethink our knee-jerk response to this issue—to attach rather than detach, to engage rather than disengage.

WHY IT MATTERS

Despite the public's increasing distrust of us, the news media are still the closest society has to any sort of public record. As Berns notes in *Framing the Victim*:

For many issues, people use the media as their *only* resource for thinking about social problems. This is not surprising if you just look around. Think of the easy access we have to television, radio, newspapers, movies, internet, books, and magazines. From these resources, individuals construct their own conceptions of what is normal and acceptable.[17]

And even if fewer people are reading newspapers or watching the news these days, the "assumption of the public presence" gives power to the media, says noted press scholar Michael Schudson. He explains that if the information is publicly available, politicians, judges, and other types of public officials "have to behave *as if* someone in the public is paying attention." They must respond to what runs in the news. As a result, the news media have enormous power in setting local or national agendas. "When the media offer the public an item of news, they confer upon it public legitimacy," Schudson says.[18]

Of course, the link between how the media frame violence and how the public responds to it is difficult to prove, but several recent studies attempt to do so. In 2008 psychologist Renae Franiuk and three other researchers conducted two studies involving news coverage of the Kobe Bryant case, and they made some important discoveries about how the presence of rape myths ("she's lying" or "she wanted it" being the most common ones) in news stories influenced people's perceptions of Bryant's guilt or innocence.

To give some background, in July 2003, a woman told Colorado authorities that Bryant, a Los Angeles Lakers basketball player, had sexually assaulted her in his hotel room. Bryant claimed the sex was consensual, but the district attorney decided there was enough evidence to charge Bryant with one count of felony sexual assault. Franiuk and her team chose to examine the news coverage of the Bryant case because it was high-profile and, as a result, had the potential to influence public opinion about sexual assault in general.

In their first study, the researchers examined 156 articles about the case from across the country, starting from when the story first broke and ending when the charges against Bryant were dropped in September 2004. They found that 65 percent of the articles included at least one rape myth-endorsing statement, with some having as many as fifteen. In the second study, the researchers tried to determine what impact such myths had on people's particular beliefs about the case. Participants were randomly assigned to read one of two fictitious articles about the incident. The first endorsed certain rape myths, while the other challenged them. For instance, the first article stated that the alleged victim was flirtatious with Bryant and "admitted to willingly kissing him," while the second mentioned that such statements "do not imply that she indeed wanted *sex.*" Not surprisingly, those who read the first article were more likely to believe Bryant's version of the events, while those who read the second were more likely to side with the woman.[19]

In summarizing their findings, the researchers speculate that rape myths, given their obvious sway over public opinion, may be partly to blame for the reluctance of most sexual assault victims to press charges—and the reluctance of judges and juries to convict those accused of the crime.[20] According to the U.S. Department of Justice, rape is still the most unreported crime in America, with just 40 percent of its victims going to the police.[21] And of those who do come forward, few will see their rapist sent to prison due to historically low conviction rates for sexual assault. Franiuk and her team note the final outcome of the Bryant case, for instance: "By her own admission, the alleged victim in this case was no longer willing to testify in the criminal trial after a year of being vilified by the press." According to the woman's lawyers, she did not think she would get a fair trial after all the media coverage of her case—an assumption, the researchers note, that their findings supported. "We will never know what specific role the media's saturation with rape myths played in the alleged victim's decision, but given the research presented here, we can fairly confidently cite negative repercussions," say Franiuk and her team. "And more important, we will never know the full impact that this case will have on future sexual assault victims and perpetrators."[22]

NOT EITHER/OR

In a recent article in *Columbia Journalism Review*, Brent Cunningham says that the goal of journalistic objectivity has persisted because "we'd like to think it buoys our embattled credibility," but he and others question whether this is actually true.[23] Indeed, if recent surveys are any indication, the U.S. news media's credibility problems are only getting worse, despite our best attempts to portray ourselves as neutral observers. According to a 2005 survey by the Pew Research Center for the People and the Press, public skepticism of the media has risen dramatically over the last twenty years, partly due to suspicions of bias. In one striking example, the number of Americans who said they could believe most of what they read in their daily paper dropped from 84 percent in 1985 to 54 percent in 2004. What's more, six in ten of those Americans surveyed saw news organizations as politically biased, up from 53 percent two years before, while seven in ten (or 72 percent) said these organizations tended to favor one side rather than treat all sides fairly—the largest number yet to express such an opinion in the survey.[24] This means that, as Eric Alterman contends in a recent issue of the *New Yorker*, "vastly more Americans believe in flying saucers and 9/11 conspiracy theories than believe in the notion of balanced—much less 'objective'—mainstream news media."[25]

In addition to sagging credibility, the news media face sagging circulation problems, again partly due to public perceptions of bias.[26] Media bloggers across the nation are wringing their hands over what appears to be the doomed fate of such journalistic giants as the *New York Times* and the *Boston Globe*; some major newspapers already have folded while others cling to life. No doubt, many factors are contributing to this downward trend—the migration of classified ads to the Web, for instance, and access to free content on the Internet—but that doesn't mean we shouldn't examine our overall mission as journalists as part of the equation. In his book *What Are Journalists For?* Jay Rosen argues for a new model of journalism known as "public journalism," which stresses citizen involvement and public discourse on important issues of the day. While this is different from what I am advocating in this book, his reasons for suggesting such a model are similar to my own. The traditional, objective news mode "failed to prevent journalism from losing its audience, losing public trust, losing effectiveness—in general losing its way," he maintains, so why continue to cling to it as the answer to the profession's woes?[27]

In challenging the objective approach to reporting, I am not suggesting journalists should focus only on their feelings when covering violence. This would tip the balance too far in the other direction. As psychiatrist and trauma expert Frank Ochberg tells me, "On the face of it, any professional who deals with vexing problems should be aware of emotion—his or her own emotion, the emotion experienced by others, and the way emotion affects reason. But awareness of emotion may become preoccupation with emotion or escalation of emotion." And this can lead to a diminishing of one's professional capacity—a blurring of one's vision. "Accuracy is critical," says Ochberg. "The instrument of news-gathering, a reporter's keen eye, must be clear."

In questioning the value of journalistic objectivity, I also am not advocating that we give up our quest for evidence as part of our research. As sociologist Kersti Yllo told me in an interview two years ago, as reporters, we still need to back up our stories with proof that is "verifiable in the empirical world." Otherwise, she says, it's the people with power who shape the news—the politicians and CEOs with the clout and cash to make their voices heard. "The only way to challenge power is with critiques based on evidence," says Yllo. "If we toss that out, power will win and dominate the airwaves."

But rather than have journalism be "either/or"—all facts or all emotions—I maintain that the news media's job is to mediate between this external empirical world and our own inner subjectivities—to interpret reality for our audiences. And tapping into our emotions can be a crucial part of this. As an example, Yllo talks about the women she interviewed for a study on marital rape. "Women described terrible experiences, and some of them hit me much harder than others, even though they were all terrible in various ways," she says. A self-described feminist sociologist, Yllo found herself reacting most strongly to those stories in which women were "socially entrapped." "It wasn't the psychotic husband who tortured his wife—that's one psychotic guy that needs to be put away. What got me so much more were these women who were trying and having to make choices between only bad options in their lives, like you're going to prostitute yourself or your child," she says. "When I saw that happening and how these women were being blamed as individuals for making bad choices, it helped to take time to figure out why I was reacting the way I was."

Sociologist Sherryl Kleinman refers to her gut-level reactions to her research as her "twinge-o-meter"—an alarm that sounds when something doesn't feel quite right. She mentions a study she once conducted in the 1980s on a holistic health center called Renewal. As she interviewed the center's staff, almost all of whom were women and underpaid (or, in some cases, not paid at all), Kleinman's twinge-o-meter kept going off. At times, she was angry with the women, wondering why they weren't angry with the center's practitioners, the majority of whom were men and apparently making good money. At first, Kleinman wanted to ignore her anger, or "twinge"—to avoid any type of feeling that would seem antagonistic toward the study's participants. But she came to realize that her anger helped her "sense" that something wasn't quite right at the center—that there were gender inequalities that needed to be explored. This inspired Kleinman to ask more probing questions of the staff and practitioners about the way they'd organized the center. "In my analysis of Renewal I came to ask: How did these women and men, with good intentions, manage not to see the ways they contradicted their own ideals?" she says. "How did they manage to maintain a belief in themselves as good people—those committed to 'alternative' ideals—despite their unfair behaviors and hierarchical organizational structure?"[28]

Eventually, Kleinman saw her emotions as a valuable piece of evidence in her research. They were not the "final word" on the holistic center, she says, but a "resource" that needed to be put to "empirical tests." In this way, Kleinman balanced her subjectivities with a more objective, scientific approach.

Yllo urges social scientists to "consider what parts of the scientific method are of value" but also to allow for "more self-reflection and criticism of our assumptions about knowledge [and] the issue of objectivity."[29] In a similar way, I maintain that in journalism, the objective should not be pitted against the subjective when writing about emotional topics like violence. Rather, the reporters I interviewed attempted to work in the gray area between the two. Feeling their way between these dual worlds, they were constantly redefining the boundaries between themselves and their subjectivities. Sometimes they had to take a step forward and plunge more deeply into their emotions in order to comprehend a story on a deeper level. Other times they had to step away from their feelings and clear their heads in order to see the complete picture. However, journalism is not a science, they told me, but a collision of human thoughts and feelings. While they were never able to completely resolve the tension between their inner and outer worlds, in creating a dialogue between them, they felt they'd inched closer to truth.

NOTES

1. John W. Heeren and Jill Theresa Messing, "Victims and Sources: Newspaper Reports of Mass Murder in Domestic Contexts," in *Women, Violence, and the Media: Readings in Feminist Criminology*, ed. Drew Humphries (Boston: Northeastern University Press, 2009), 206–7.

2. Stephen J. Berry, "Why Objectivity Still Matters," *Nieman Reports* 59.2 (Summer 2005): 15.

3. Susan Krieger, *Social Science and the Self: Personal Essays on an Art Form* (New Brunswick, N.J.: Rutgers University Press, 1991), 1.

4. Krieger, *Social Science and the Self*, 32.

5. Eric Alterman, "'Objectivity RIP,'" *Nation*, December 24, 2001, 12.

6. Drew Humphries, "Gendered Constructions: Women and Violence," *Women, Violence, and the Media*, 23, 24.

7. Cathy Ferrand Bullock and Jason Cubert, "Coverage of Domestic Violence Fatalities by Newspapers in Washington State," *Journal of Interpersonal Violence* 17, no. 5 (May 2002): 475–99.

8. Marian Meyers, *News Coverage of Domestic Violence: Engendering Blame* (Thousand Oaks, Calif.: Sage Publications, Inc. 1997), 122.

9. Bullock and Cubert, "Coverage of Domestic Violence Fatalities by Newspapers in Washington State," 490, 493.

10. Meyers, *News Coverage of Violence Against Women*, 66.

11. James W. Carey, "Why and How? The Dark Continent of American Journalism," in *Reading the News: A Pantheon Guide to Popular Culture*, ed. Robert Karl Manoff and Michael Schudson (New York: Pantheon Books, 1996), 167.

12. Carey, "Why and How? The Dark Continent of American Journalism," 180.

13. Nancy Berns, *Framing the Victim: Domestic Violence, Media and Social Problems* (New York: Aldine de Gruyter, 2004), 6, 31.

14. Meyers, *News Coverage of Violence Against Women*, 86–88, 99, 101.

15. Michelle L. Meloy and Susan L. Miller, "Words That Wound," *Women, Violence, and the Media*, 32–40.

16. Meyers, *News Coverage of Violence Against Women*, 98.

17. Berns, *Framing the Victim*, 35.

18. Michael Schudson, *The Power of News* (Cambridge, Mass.: Harvard University Press, 1995), 19, 25.

19. Renae Franiuk et al., "Prevalence and Effects of Rape Myths in Print Journalism," *Violence Against Women* 14, no. 3 (2008): 288, 292–93, 296–98.

20. Franiuk et al., "Prevalence and Effects of Rape Myths in Print Journalism," 290.

21. Michael Rand and Shannon Catalano, "Criminal Victimization, 2006," *Bureau of Justice Statistics Bulletin* (December 2007).

22. Franiuk et al., "Prevalence and Effects of Rape Myths in Print Journalism," 301, 303.

23. Brent Cunningham, "Toward a New Ideal: Re-thinking Objectivity in a World of Spin," *Columbia Journalism Review* (July/August 2003).

24. The Pew Research Center for People & the Press, "Public More Critical of Press, but Goodwill Persists," June 26, 2005, people-press.org/report/248/public-more-critical-of-press-but-goodwill-persists (accessed September 12, 2008).

25. Eric Alterman, "Out of Print: The Death and Life of the American Newspaper," *New Yorker*, March 31, 2008.

26. Project for Excellence in Journalism, *State of the News Media 2007: An Annual Report on American Journalism*, 2007.

27. Jay Rosen, *What Are Journalists For?* (New Haven, Conn.: Yale University Press, 1999), 183.

28. Sherryl Kleinman, "Feminist Fieldwork Analysis," *Qualitative Research Methods Series* 51 (Thousand Oaks, Calif: Sage Publications, Inc., 2007), 2, 5.

29. Kersti Yllo, "Political and Methodological Debates in Wife Abuse Research," *Feminist Perspectives on Wife Abuse*, ed. Kersti Yllo and Michele Bograd (Newbury Park, Calif: Sage Publications, Inc., 1998), 35, 48.

2

❧

Getting Engaged

The History of Emotional Reporting

In 1936 James Agee and Walker Evans traveled to Alabama for *Fortune* magazine to report on the lives of poor white sharecroppers. Four years earlier, Agee had arrived at *Fortune* straight out of Harvard, and right from the start, this brash, young journalist had resisted the conventions of his trade. "Who, what, where, when, and why (or how) is the primal cliché and complacency of journalism." Agee wrote in *Let Us Now Praise Famous Men*, his tormented masterpiece chronicling his trip to the South.[1] In his collaboration with Evans, Agee wanted to move beyond the just-the-facts approach to reporting. He wanted to get to know the families he profiled—the Gudgers, Ricketts, and Woods—on a more intimate level. It was hard work.

About a month into the assignment, Agee was frustrated. He felt that he and Evans "had not as yet found anything which could satisfy our hope, our need, our determination to do truly." Everything changed the day a storm blew in on Hobe's Hill, where the three families he was profiling lived. Holed up in their rundown shack, the Gudgers gave Agee shelter. When the last of the rain had fallen, George Gudger invited him to stay the night, but Agee politely refused in what he later described as "some paralyzing access of shyness before strong desire."

Driving away, he chided himself for refusing Gudger's offer—"sure, and sick to hell, that I had hurt him, that I had seemed in my refusal to set myself above him." As chance would have it (or perhaps as Agee himself had willed it), his car got stuck in a ditch not far from the Gudgers' home. Not at all upset by this turn of events, Agee promptly changed into his sneakers, rolled up his pants, and trudged back to the shack. For Agee, the night he spent with the Gudgers was the turning point in his relationship with the family. George and his wife, Annie Mae, fed him supper—fried pork, eggs, field peas, and warmed over biscuits—and by the light of the fire Agee and his hosts got to know one another. In *Let Us Now Praise Famous Men*, he described their emerging sense of kinship:

> [T]here is a particular sort of intimacy between the three of us which is not of our creating and which has nothing to do with our talk, yet which is increased in our tones of voice, in small quiet turns of humor, in glances of the eyes, in ways even that I eat my food, in their knowledge how truly friendly I feel toward them.[2]

Clearly, Agee had no qualms about forming a relationship with his subjects. In fact, he considered it an essential part of his reporting. What's more, he was not afraid to tap into his emotions during the course of his reporting, and his book oozes with the anger and guilt he felt over the social injustices he witnessed in the South.

At times, Agee also felt an overwhelming sense of shame for prying into the lives of an "undefended and appallingly damaged group of human beings," and he fervently hoped that no harm would come to the people about whom he wrote. Agee was not afraid to step down from his neutral perch and emotionally *attach* himself to his subjects. That meant relating to them in human terms. For Agee, it was the only way. Referring to George Gudger, he wrote, "I know him only so far as I know him, and only in those terms in which I know him; and all of that depends as fully on who I am as on who he is."[3]

While Agee was one of the first American journalists to practice what I consider emotionally engaged reporting (I also see glimpses of it in the nonfiction work of Stephen Crane and Jack London), he certainly would not be the last. In fact, this type of journalism would not have its heyday until the 1960s, when Vietnam—and the generational rebellion that accompanied it—would give reporters permission to express their feelings as never before. As I will explore in this chapter, such turning points in U.S. history—Vietnam, World War II, the fight for civil rights, and most recently, Hurricane Katrina—brought emotionally engaged reporting to the fore. The moral urgency of people suffering and dying inspired countless journalists at least temporarily to choose passion and outrage over neutrality. These journalists knew that "on the one hand this/on the other hand that" type of reporting wouldn't cut it—wouldn't change enough minds to make a difference. Their allegiances shifted from staying true to the tenets of their profession to staying true to their consciences, to their own sense of justice.

During these intense periods in American history, journalism mattered more than at any other time; lives hung in the balance and these reporters knew it. As a result, it would have been morally wrong for them *not* to have felt a personal connection to their work. In his book *People's Witness: The Journalist in Modern Politics*, Fred Inglis mentions conflict reporter Martha Gellhorn, famous for her compassionate dispatches from the front lines during World War II. He says:

> [I]f some crazy priest of journalism were to criticize her for so clearly report-ing from one side (difficult, of course, at that time to report on the other) and failing to take the high view from nowhere, one could only rejoin on her part that such a precept was and remains morally mad, cognitively unfeasible, and humanly repulsive.[4]

This more personal style of journalism certainly never replaced the objec-tive model at any point in history. Rather, emotionally engaged reporting challenged the basic rules of the profession at pivotal moments, when the stakes were high. Once a crisis had passed, the majority of journalists seemed to revert to their more neutral ways, perhaps because it was easier to put aside their feelings during these more stable periods.

But those reporters who did voice an opinion or emotion during times of war or social upheaval ultimately had a profound impact on their audi-ences. In taking a stand, they signaled to the rest of the world that a stand needed to be taken. If journalists, who were supposed to be neutral, were expressing outrage or despair, then surely the situation was a dire one in-deed. These reporters sounded the alarm when it was crucial they do so.

THE ROOTS OF PERSONAL JOURNALISM

The American news media's first experiences with emotionally engaged reporting actually stretch back centuries. According to journalism scholar Michael Schudson, the first hint of passion in the press came during the American Revolution. During such a divided time, it was almost taboo for the press *not* to take sides. "As conflict with Britain heated up after 1765, politics entered the press and printerly 'fairness' went by the board," says Schudson in *The Sociology of News*. Prior to this, colonial newspapers had stayed far away from politics to avoid the wrath of local authorities. Schud-son explains that, during the first half-century of American journalism, from about 1690 to the 1760s, "America had a very different understand-ing of a free press and a very strong sense of government as a precarious entity." As a result, newspaper proprietors who criticized the government often were indicted for libel as a way to maintain political order.[5]

But all this changed during the American Revolution. Suddenly, print shops were "hives of political activity," says Schudson, and political pam-phleteers were pounding the pavement in big cities like Boston and Philadelphia. In 1776, this type of political activity reached its peak with the publication of Thomas Paine's *Common Sense*—a plainspoken, passionate plea against British rule that sold an estimated 150,000 copies.[6] "Everything that is right or reasonable pleads for separation," Paine wrote. "The blood of the slain, the weeping voice of nature cries, 'Tis time to part.'"[7]

Over the next two centuries, the news media would undergo an identity crisis of sorts, bouncing between detachment and more emotionally and politically engaged reporting in response to the times. During the mid-nineteenth century, the rise of the so-called penny papers resulted in journalism's first step toward the more facts-based model of journalism we see today. Rather than being available by subscription only to an elite readership, the penny papers were hawked on the streets for a mere cent to anyone who would buy them. At the time, more people had access to the growing economy and thus to wealth and political power, and the penny papers capitalized on this. To appeal to as many readers as possible (which, in turn, would attract advertisers), the papers' editors abandoned political editorials in favor of more local news from the police, courts, and society in general. They stayed focused on the facts, distrusting, as Schudson says, "the reality, or objectivity, of 'values.'"[8]

Over the next few decades, this more objective approach to journalism would blossom into a full-blown ideal in response to two other trends. The first and perhaps most significant was America's increasing reverence for science as the "new religion" of the times. This resulted in an overall sense that "the world was knowable and nameable ("naïve empiricism"), if only we roll up our sleeves and investigate it," says press historian David Mindich.[9]

A third trend that pushed the news media in the direction of objectivity was the introduction of public relations in the early twentieth century. During World War I, President Woodrow Wilson unknowingly had helped inspire this new industry by waging various campaigns to sell the war to the American public. His efforts were so successful that by 1920, almost a thousand bureaus of propaganda had sprung up in Washington, D.C. Bombarded with PR, the news media began to see how malleable the "facts" really were, how they could be "created" by special interests with the power and money to wage campaigns.[10] As Schudson notes of this post-war era, "Journalists had rejected parties only to discover their newfound independence besieged by information mercenaries hired by government, business, politicians, and others."[11]

To resist these forces of spin control, the press adopted a kind of aggressive professionalism in which everything and everyone was suspect. The ideal of journalistic objectivity—of divorcing oneself from one's emotions and personal biases—became a clearly defined ideal among the news media. But as Schudson points out, this ideal seemed to unravel almost as soon as it was formulated. By the 1930s and 1940s, readers were craving interpretation in response to increasingly complex times. "The idea is that the war, the depression, and then the New Deal made political, economic, and social affairs so complicated that they forced journalism to emphasize the 'meaning' of the news and the context of events," Schudson contends.[12]

World War II also provided the ideal moral backdrop for journalists to take more of a personal stand in their reporting. Several of them stood out in this regard, including Ernie Pyle and the previously mentioned Gellhorn. But perhaps no one embodied this notion of emotionally engaged reporting more than CBS broadcaster Edward R. Murrow. In his coverage of World War II and, later, McCarthyism, Murrow helped change the nature of his profession from one of passively reporting the facts to actively grappling with the subject matter. Like Agee, Murrow was not afraid to voice his anger at the injustices he witnessed—and to make his audiences uncomfortable in the process. In this Christmas Eve broadcast in 1940, Murrow urged his fellow Americans not to be complacent as Hitler hammered away at the British:

> This is not a merry Christmas in London. I heard that phrase only twice in the last three days. This afternoon as the stores were closing, as shoppers and office workers were hurrying home, one heard such phrases as "So long, Mamie" and "Good luck, Jack" but never "A merry Christmas."[13]

Murrow has been called a pioneer of broadcast journalism. It is certainly true that he showed American audiences just how powerful the mediums of radio and television could be. His reports for CBS conveyed an immediacy of time and place like never before, and for the first time, he proved that a journalist could be more than the sum of his or her words on the page.

During his wartime broadcasts, people could hear the emotion in his voice, which cracked on more than one occassion. In this broadcast three days after American troops liberated the Nazi concentration camp at Buchenwald, Murrow openly acknowledged his presence at the scene:

> There surged around me an evil-smelling horde. Men and boys reached out to touch me; they were in rags and the remnants of uniform. Death had already marked many of them, but they were smiling with their eyes. I looked out over that mass of men to the green fields beyond where well-fed Germans were plowing.[14]

Anonymous no more, Murrow abandoned the traditional third-person type of reporting for something more personal. He refused to be the kind of journalist who closed himself off from the world while those around him suffered. While in London during World War II, for instance, he "avoided bomb shelters except to report about them," says one of his biographers, and he drove through the streets in an open car.[15]

Murrow was best known, though, for brazenly challenging authority, particularly during the era of McCarthyism in the 1950s. Indeed, while many of his colleagues merely chronicled Senator McCarthy's lies and accusations without comment, Murrow openly opposed them. In covering the senator, he was one of the first U.S reporters to embrace the model of advocacy journalism—to let his emotions inform his work to the point where he was willing to take a stand. Murrow crossed over into television in 1951, and his show, *See It Now*, was just about a month old when it first reported on McCarthy. In one of his most famous reports, Murrow ended the 1954 broadcast with this warning: "We proclaim ourselves, as indeed we are, defenders of freedom—what's left of it—but we cannot defend freedom abroad by deserting it at home."

Murrow would pay a price for investing so much of himself in his work. Less than two months after that 1954 broadcast, *See It Now* lost its sponsor (which did not want to be linked with an apparent Communist sympathizer) and its prime-time spot. Relegated to Sundays, *See It Now* was cancelled four years later. Murrow was crushed.[16] A disillusioned man, he died just two days after his fifty-seventh birthday in 1965. His intense commitment to his work had driven him to a point of physical and emotional exhaustion. Murrow's impact on the practice of journalism cannot be underestimated. In *People's Witness*, Inglis describes the broadcaster's reporting as from a different source than most—from deeply held convictions rather than mere facts. Inglis contends:

> Freedom, you might say, was for a man like Murrow . . . the practice of virtue itself. The freely speaking man not only treats ideas as the grammar of his motives to act well, but in so practicing his freedom of speech and therefore action, treats the exchange of ideas as the innately democratic and necessarily courteous business of public life, without which the arena of the polity is abandoned to the care of the gun and the rat.[17]

Some might say Murrow stepped too far out of the bounds of journalism, but I would disagree. He passionately believed in such constitutional ideals as free speech, and when he saw those ideals threatened by the likes of McCarthy, he shed his role as a passive observer and acted, at great cost to himself.

It would be easy to say that the notion of journalistic objectivity was forever altered thanks to Ed Murrow. But as Schudson points out in *Discovering the News: A Sociological History of American Newspapers*, while many other U.S. reporters during the McCarthy era were "angry that the conventions of their work required them to publish 'news' they knew to be false," they had yet to reject these conventions outright.[18] When Murrow signed off for the last time on *See It Now* in 1958, many journalists were still sorting through the mixed signals of their profession. While news commentators/reporters like Murrow and political columnists like Walter Lippmann were now widely accepted as their audiences' guides through the rapids of the times, many daily news journalists still adhered to the same old style of neutral reporting, always being sure to get "both sides" of every story.

It would take years of having their idealism shattered—by the government's lies in Vietnam and the atrocities they witnessed there—before these journalists began to change their views. In his Pulitzer Prize-winning book about Vietnam, *A Bright Shining Lie*, Neil Sheehan describes the war as not just a turning point for journalists but for all Americans. He says, "[T]he generation of the 1950s . . . was the last generation of Americans to go so naively into the world. It was destined to lose its innocence in the war and be forced to grapple with the consequences of disillusionment."[19]

Over time, this disillusionment would grow so intense that the news media would began to see the objectivity-at-any-cost model of journalism as an almost evil force within their profession—a force that promoted the viewpoints of liars and cheats. But when David Halberstam arrived in Vietnam in 1962, American disillusionment still was far from a reality. Halberstam embodied the naïve enthusiasm still so prominent within his generation. A twenty-eight-year-old reporter from New York, he stood over six feet tall and was known to gesture wildly with his oversized hands. He has been described as a powder keg, a man with a fire in his belly who was "full of opinions and full of himself."[20] He could be impatient and quick to anger, but like Murrow and Agee, he used these qualities as a positive force in his work.[21]

His capacity for anger, particularly at any kind of social injustice, can be traced to two distinct periods in his life—his childhood and his coverage of the early civil rights movement in the South. Halberstam was born in 1934 in New York City. He and his family moved often as his father struggled as a young doctor during the Depression. Always the new kids in town, David and his brother, Michael, often had to prove themselves in the schoolyard, using their fists to do so. Tragically, Halberstam's father died when David was just sixteen, and his mother moved the family to Connecticut, where she worked as a schoolteacher.[22] Both sets of David's grandparents were Jewish immigrants, and throughout his life, Halberstam felt an "enduring sense of Jewish apartness," says Sheehan, who speculates that this may have been what drove his intense ambition.[23]

But Halberstam was not one for self-analysis, according to William Prochnau, who interviewed the former *New York Times* writer for his book

Once Upon a Distant War. Halberstam once told Prochnau, "So I was the only Jewish kid in a small town in the 1950s. So I fought in the schoolyard. . . . But the anger mostly came out of the bullshit. It was the lies. It should make anyone angry." Halberstam felt fortunate to have found a profession in which he could use his anger, his "psychological given," in such a positive way, he told Prochnau. His anger made him rebel against and question authority, and this was not a bad trait to have in the 1960s. [24]

After graduating from Harvard in 1955, Halberstam's anger was primed even more during the five years he spent writing about the early civil rights movement in the South. To the astonishment of many of his Harvard classmates, he'd taken a job at Mississippi's smallest daily newspaper. The Harvard grad had been eager to dive right into the South's racial problems, but his ambition was soon thwarted by a publisher who was not very interested in such controversial stories. Halberstam was fired just seven months after arriving at the paper.[25]

He soon landed on his feet, though, at the *Nashville Tennessean*, where he began writing the race-related stories he'd so wanted to cover in Mississippi. During his four years with the paper, his aggressive coverage of the burgeoning civil rights movement helped give its leaders a sense of legitimacy. In some of his more famous reports, he followed a group of young black students known as the Nashville Movement as they led lunch-counter sit-ins in that city in 1960. To anyone who read his stories, it was clear where Halberstam stood: racism was morally wrong. He had no qualms about taking such a definitive stand. "It was a great story—one set of Americans trying to deny rights of another set of Americans," he told one newspaper reporter in 1999. "The editorial bias is not in the reporting, the bias is in the ugliness of the act."[26]

After Halberstam's death in an automobile accident in 2007, Georgia Representative John Lewis, a former member of the Nashville Movement, talked about how Halberstam had been a dear friend and compatriot in the struggle for civil rights. In a statement to the press, Lewis said Halberstam "was deeply moved and affected by the discipline, the commitment, and the dedication of the young people in the Nashville Movement because they were prepared to face violence with non-violence and peace."[27]

Halberstam would apply this same passion, this same sense of justice, to the war in Vietnam, but this time for the *New York Times*, where he began working in 1961. From the start, some of the paper's editors were less than thrilled to be working with this volatile young reporter. In *Once Upon A Distant War*, Prochneau explains that when Halberstam first started writing for the paper, the *Times* "was just beginning to emerge from a period in which it had become unusually hidebound, almost like the medieval church." The paper had rules and strict notions about objectivity, and Halberstam, true to form, rebelled against them.[28]

COUNTERCULTURALISM AND NEW JOURNALISM

Halberstam was giving voice to an emerging trend within his profession—the idea that journalism was not living up to its full potential and had to move beyond dry, lifeless reporting. Of course, he and his colleagues at the time had differing opinions on just where journalism needed to go. At the *Washington Post*, a young reporter named Tom Wolfe was experimenting more with style than content as a way to liven up his reporting. Nonfiction writers, he said, were supposed to write in a "calm, cultivated, and . . . genteel voice," a voice "like the off-white or putty-colored walls that Syrie Maugham popularized in interior decoration . . . a 'neutral background' against which bits of color would stand out." Readers were "bored to tears" by such stories, claimed Wolfe, who was advocating for a more literary style of journalism in which real-life subjects became characters in richly told stories.[29] At the time, Halberstam and Wolfe did not realize just how large a media revolution they were participating in—or how strong the zeitgeist they were expressing.

As Sheehan points out, Vietnam robbed Americans of a certain innocence, of a naïve faith that the world was knowable and predictable. Reporters on the ground were measuring what the government was telling them against what they were witnessing with their own eyes, and it was clear the authorities were lying to them. What would weaken their and most Americans' sense of security even more was the assassination of President John F. Kennedy in 1963. In perhaps the most emotional moment of any journalist captured on television, Walter Cronkite broke into daily programming on November 22, 1963, to tell viewers that the president had been shot. Removing and replacing his thick glasses as he peered up at the clock and recounted the time of death, Cronkite struggled to keep his composure. "An understandable world was coming apart at the 'seems'—appearances could not be trusted," Schduson contends. He is referring not only to the death of John Kennedy but the later assassinations of Kennedy's brother, Robert, and of Martin Luther King Jr.[30]

The revelations of the Pentagon Papers and Watergate just a few years later would only add to the public's distrust of authorities and its overall sense that the world was unraveling into chaos. Over time, a culture of criticism took root in the United States as a way for people to challenge those in power and take back some sense of control. In journalism, this culture manifested itself in two ways—in the muckraking style of reporting that resulted in Watergate and in the trend known as New Journalism.[31] While there is no official definition of New Journalism, there were certain characteristics that its practitioners seemed to share. They wanted to do more than provide a factual account of the complex events unfolding around them. Like the counterculturalists of the 1960s, they were subversive and anti-establishment in that they rejected the rules of their trade as outdated and ineffectual. They experimented with inserting themselves in their stories as a way to help interpret the world for their readers. With a disdain for authorities and their "facts," many New Journalists openly embraced their subjectivities in their stories, believing it was as close as their audiences would get to truth.

In *The Gang That Wouldn't Write Straight*, Marc Weingarten talks about the rise of this new form of journalism.

> Within a seven-year period, a group of writers emerged, seemingly out of nowhere . . . to impose some order on all of this American mayhem, each in his or her own distinctive manner. . . . They came to tell us stories about ourselves in ways that we couldn't, stories about the way life was being lived in the sixties and seventies and what it all meant. The stakes were high; deep fissures were rending the social fabric, the world was out of order. So they became our master explainers, our town criers, even our moral conscience—the New Journalists.[32]

Wolfe was perhaps the most visible (and vocal) embodiment of this. He was a zealous practitioner of the form with such zany masterpieces as *The Electric Kool-Aid Acid Test* about Ken Kesey and his band of Merry Pranksters. But Wolfe was clear about his intentions. He was interested in refining his technique—not altering the nature of the profession overall. New Journalism, he maintained, was not subjective journalism. It was not simply a matter of the author inserting him or herself into his or her stories. It also was not political, even though many liberal reporters used it to convey their opposition to the Vietnam War. For Wolfe, New Journalism was the novelistic rendering of factual stories—a way to give readers "the feeling of being inside the character's mind and experiencing the emotional reality of the scene as he experiences it."[33]

Over time, though, Wolfe's definition would be challenged by other writers who were experimenting with this new form as well. They tested its limits—how far could they go with their experimentation and still call it journalism? "Wolfe's problem," New Journalist Hunter S. Thompson once wrote, "is that he's too crusty to participate in his stories."[34] Thompson, on the other hand, did not hesitate to immerse and include himself in his stories. In one of his more notorious excursions, he was once beat up by a group of Hell's Angels as part of his initiation into the group. For Thompson and other New Journalists, the subjective voice served a purpose. A new era in American politics and culture required a new kind of journalism, a way to challenge the nation's timidity and its false respect for authority. The neutral, reserved voice of the conventional reporter simply did not have the power to do that.

The New Journalists also didn't trust the rhetoric of objectivity to capture the complexities of the times. When Norman Mailer set out to chronicle the 1967 antiwar march on the Pentagon in his book *The Armies of the Night*, he abandoned journalistic conventions for a more novelistic style. He made himself a protagonist in his own story, comically referring to himself in the third person as "Mailer," "the Novelist," and "our General." The book, which bears the subtitles "The Novel as History" and "History as a Novel," recounts Mailer's own participation in the march—how he was arrested for crossing a police line and how he'd become so drunk at an event prior to the march that he'd urinated on the men's room floor.

In his book, Mailer explains why he embraced the novel as the means by which he told his story. The history of the march, he said, was inherently personal: "[N]o documents can give sufficient intimation: the novel must replace history at precisely that point where experience is sufficiently emotional, spiritual, psychical, moral, existential, or supernatural."[35] By making himself a character in his nonfiction novel, Mailer was able to embody the pent-up angst and frustration of his generation—and younger ones as well. At the same time, because he referred to himself in the third person, he maintained some of the distance of a journalist. In a 1968 review of the book in the *New York Times*, Alfred Kazin wrote, "For all his self-dramatization, Mailer is the right chronicler of the March on the Pentagon. For there is no writer of his ability who, feeling so deeply about this 'obscene war . . . the worst war the nation has ever been in,' can yet be so aware of everything else around him."[36]

Relieved of what Kazin described as "vexing dualities,"[37] Mailer was able to take the best of both worlds—the subjective and the objective—and capture an extraordinary moment in time. His critics say he never wrote anything nearly as brilliant again, a contention with which even Mailer seemed to agree. In an interview with the *New York Times* in 1982, he explained how the moral urgency of the 1960s—Vietnam and the fight for civil rights—had inspired him as a writer. Over time, though, the idealism of the radical left began to wane as political realities set in, and Mailer felt less and less inspired, realizing that his writing was not making as much of a difference as he'd hoped.[38]

In *The Gang That Wouldn't Write Straight*, Weingarten says the "ideological breakdowns of the sixties were a bitter disappointment" to the likes of Mailer and other journalists who "truly believed that they just might bear witness to a great American political awakening." Instead, says Weingarten, "Nixon was reelected" and "the New Left splintered and faded."[39] In his 1982 interview with the *Times*, Mailer characterized the 1970s by the "lack of ideas that anyone was even remotely willing to die for." He said he had "lost all the easy optimism about how quickly one could affect things in the world as a writer."[40] Mailer also had grown weary of writing about himself. He began producing books about celebrities like Marilyn Monroe, Henry Miller, and Muhammad Ali. In doing so, he shifted away from New Journalism toward a more objective style of writing, signaling the end of the radical movement that had redefined, albeit briefly, the nature of journalism.

HISTORY REPEATING ITSELF?

After the 1960s, New Journalism didn't so much die as peter out, and traces of it and other writing styles from that era remain. Muckraking, for instance, has become a permanent fixture in journalism, incorporated under the heading of "investigative reporting" and expertly executed by the likes of the *New Yorker*'s Seymour Hersh and the *New York Times*' Walter Bogdanich. The narrative style of journalism also is alive and well, with reporters picking and choosing those novelistic techniques that work for their stories. However, the more personally engaged style of reporting by Halberstam, Murrow, and Mailer does not exist as a full-fledged movement anymore. We have seen flashes of it—in Anderson Cooper's reports on Hurricane Katrina, for instance—but it is usually cordoned off as a "type" of journalism rather than its mission. Is it that this type of intense, emotionally charged writing is not sustainable, that those reporters who use it all the time inevitably will burn out? Or is it that to employ this more passionate style of writing on a regular basis would lessen its impact—that we need to save our firepower for when it's really necessary? Why do some situations—World War II and the civil rights movement, for instance—bring out more emotionally engaged reporting while others, like the Iraq War, don't?

No doubt, we live in more morally ambiguous times. War is no longer fought in the open but behind closed doors, and politicians have become even more adept at manipulating truth for their own purposes. Right and wrong have become harder to define, and viewers and readers have become accustomed to seeking confirmation of their views from like-minded politically oriented sources. They have come to expect journalists to be opinionated. Just tune in to cable pundits like Bill O'Reilly or Keith Olbermann, and you'll get an earful about the Iraq War or Afghanistan. But unlike Murrow, these news commentators seem to care more about ratings than promoting social justice, their views more outlandish than thoughtful. In addition, it is important to make a distinction between irrational (and perhaps even artificial) passion and informed, thoughtful passion. David Halberstam was, first and foremost, a brilliant reporter. His outrage stemmed from his careful study of a situation, from a painstaking process of researching every detail before forming any conclusions.

But today, outrage is almost an automatic fallback position for the likes of O'Reilly and Olbermann.

On his Comedy Central show *The Colbert Report,* Stephen Colbert takes on the persona of a pompous, blustering television pundit. He ridicules political commentators like O'Reilly, who often ignores the facts altogether in his tirades against liberals. In one of his more famous skits, Colbert riffs on the made-up word "truthiness." "The truthiness is anyone can read the news to you," he says. "I promise to feel the news at you." Colbert warns his viewers not to trust what they read in books but to listen to their guts:

> Who's Britannica to tell me that the Panama Canal was finished in 1914? If I want to say it happened in 1941, that's my right. I don't trust books. They're all facts, no heart. And that's exactly what's pulling our country apart today. . . . And what about Iraq? If you think about it, maybe there are a few missing pieces to the rationale of war. But doesn't taking Saddam out feel like the right thing, right here in the gut? Because that's where the truth comes from, ladies and gentlemen, the gut. Do you know you have more nerve endings in your stomach than in your head? Look it up. Now somebody's gonna say, 'I did look it up, and it's wrong.' Well, mister, that's because you looked it up in a book. Next time, try looking it up in your gut. I did. And my gut tells me that's how our nervous system works.[41]

Are O'Reilly and Olbermann the downside of passionate reporting—or simply a subversion of the form? Can we even include them as part of the news media, or are they a different animal altogether?

I ask the same question about bloggers, who arguably could be engaged in a more emotionally involved style of reporting. In a recent article for the *Atlantic* magazine, Andrew Sullivan argues that blogging is to writing what "extreme sports is to athletics: more free-form, more accident-prone, less formal, more alive." Because bloggers are always on deadline, with no spare time to finesse or think too much about what they write, they are more vulnerable than traditional journalists. According to Sullivan, "The wise panic that can paralyze a writer—the fear that he will be exposed, undone, humiliated—is not available to a blogger."[42]

Sullivan argues that bloggers are ushering in a "golden era in journalism," but I am not so sure—simply because I don't believe we can call them true journalists. To me, a blogger is someone who publishes online and whose work is subjected to less editorial oversight than an article that runs in print. In addition, the author's point of view is usually more prominent. But within this definition is an enormous range of writers—those who spew opinion with absolutely no regard for balance or actual reporting and those who publish more thoughtful articles based on careful research. To me, passion or personal opinion without any grounding in evidence is just as dangerous as factual reporting without emotion. I believe the key is finding a balance between the two.

In a recent *New Yorker* article examining the popularity of Keith Olbermann's in-your-face style of news, former NBC anchor Tom Brokaw describes the tension between objective reporting and subjective commentary like Olbermann's as "the second big bang" among U.S. news media. "We are creating a new universe, and it has all kinds of new laws and science and physics coming into play as well, in this information world," he says. "And you've got planets out there colliding with each other, new life forms taking shape; others have drifted too close to the sun, and they've burned up."[43] We have yet to see how the planets will realign, but clearly we are in the process, once again, of redefining journalism's role in American society.

Like the New Journalists of Tom Wolfe's era, perhaps we need to explore the extremes of this new form before it settles into something more useful and credible. Will myriad channels of twenty-four-hour anger one day pave the way for a kinder, gentler form of passion, or will it continue to scare "straight" more mainstream journalists who don't want to be labeled as biased? Right now, there is a schism between pundits like Olbermann and conventional reporters at publications like the *Times*, and my hope is that a bridge can be built between the two. We have the power to inform our subjectivities, after all, to nurture them into something more than gut reactions.

In discussing the debate in social science over quantitative versus qualitative research, sociologist Kersti Yllo warns that a "triangulation of methods" is not the solution.[44] I also believe that journalists cannot ease the tension between the subjective and objective simply by trying to be both extremes at once. Murrow and Halberstam seemed to occupy a middle ground, and journalists like Anderson Cooper and others I will profile in upcoming chapters seem to be at least attempting to reclaim this territory. I wouldn't call it a revolution but a slow migration away from objectivity to something—anything—else. The calls for a more emotionally engaged type of reporting are getting louder, with even mainstream media journals like *Columbia Journalism Review* (CJR) questioning the news media's goal of objectivity.

In his CJR article on the topic, Brent Cunningham asserts that journalism needs a revised set of instructions. One of his suggestions is that the American news media drop their objective façade and admit to their own subjectivities. "If we stop claiming to be mere objective observers," he says, "it will not end the charges of bias but will allow us to defend what we do from a more realistic, less hypocritical position."[45]

In *Just the Facts*, Mindich takes a similar position. Referring to former CBS News anchor Dan Rather, he says:

What Rather actually does offer is not reality but mediation between out there and in here. What we must ask Rather and company is that their filters be *better* than those of O'Reilly and company. What we need Rather to do is explain his filters, to tell us how he interprets reality and why we should buy his interpretation.[46]

There is no textbook for this type of reporting, but there are the writings that Agee, Murrow, Halberstam, and Mailer left behind. While New Journalism has receded, the questions it raised about objectivity versus emotionally engaged reporting linger. With our news coming from so many different sources—and those in power continually trying to manipulate it—it is no longer sufficient to report "just the facts."

During Vietnam, Halberstam stepped out of his role as a neutral reporter because he could no longer justify not taking a stand against such a morally egregious situation. He had to fight the government's complex web of lies with his own interpretation of truth. He had the courage of his convictions because he allowed himself to *have* convictions. The same could be said of Agee, Murrow, and Mailer. No doubt, they were flawed human beings, but this is precisely the point. They took a risk in their writing and reporting, and sometimes they failed. If journalism truly is to undergo a "second big bang," it probably won't be pretty. Those reporters I interviewed who admitted to a more emotional style of reporting said they'd made mistakes along the way—something journalists are not very comfortable doing given our very public role. However, as the reporters pointed out, it is only in the messy realm of uncertainty that true growth can occur.

NOTES

1. James Agee, *Let Us Now Praise Famous Men* (Boston: Houghton Mifflin, 1941), 206.

2. Agee, *Let Us Now Praise Famous Men*, 329, 358–67.

3. Agee, *Let Us Now Praise Famous Men*, 5, 211.

4. Fred Inglis, *People's Witness: The Journalist in Modern Politics* (New Haven, Conn: Yale University Press, 2002), 14.

5. Michael Schudson, *The Sociology of News* (New York: W.W. Norton & Company, Inc., 2003), 72–73.

6. Schudson, *The Sociology of News*, 73.

7. "Thomas Paine: Common Sense." American Revolution Primary Sources. UXL-GALE, 2005. eNotes.com. 2006. www.enotes.com/american-revolution-primary-sources/thomas-paine-common-sense (accessed July 1, 2009).

8. Michael Schudson, *Discovering the News: A Sociological History of American Newspapers* (New York: Basic Books, Inc., 1978), 18–22, 57–60.

9. David T. Z. Mindich, *Just the Facts: How "Objectivity" Came to Define American Journalism* (New York: New York University Press, 1998), 102.

10. Schudson, *Discovering the News*, 138.

11. Schudson, *The Sociology of News*, 83.

12. Schudson, *Discovering the News*, 146, 148.

13. Edward Bliss, Jr., ed., *In Search of the Light: The Broadcasts of Edward R. Murrow 1938–1961* (New York: Alfred A. Knopf, 1967), 43.

14. Bliss, *In Search of the Light*, 91.

15. Bob Edwards, *Edward R. Murrow and the Birth of Broadcast Journalism* (Hoboken, N.J.: John Wiley & Sons, 2004), 56.

16. Edwards, *Edward R. Murrow and the Birth of Broadcast Journalism*, 98, 106–129.

17. Inglis, *People's Witness*, 179.

18. Schudson, *Discovering the News*, 168.

19. Neil Sheehan, *A Bright Shining Lie: John Paul Vann and America in Vietnam* (New York: Vintage Books, 1989), 320.

20. William Prochnau, *Once Upon a Distant War: David Halberstam, Neil Sheehan, Peter Arnett—Young War Correspondents and Their Early Vietnam Battles* (New York: Vintage Books, 1996), 132–141.

21. Sheehan, *A Bright Shining Lie*, 319.

22. Prochnau, *Once Upon a Distant War*, 144–145.

23. Sheehan, *A Bright Shining Lie*, 318.

24. William Prochnau, "The Upside of Anger: A David Halberstam Appreciation," *American Journalism Review* (June/July 2007).

25. Prochnau, *Once Upon a Distant War*, 147.

26. Andrea Vogt, "Memories of the '60s Still Hearten Writer; Journalist David Halberstam Speaks on Civil Rights Movement," *Spokesman Review*, April 9, 1999, B1.

27. The office of Georgia Rep. John Lewis, *Rep. John Lewis on Death of Journalist David Halberstam*, State News Service, April 23, 2007.

28. Prochnau, *Once Upon a Distant War*, 137.

29. Tom Wolfe, *The New Journalism* (London: Picador, 1975), 31.

30. Schudson, *Discovering the News*, 177.

31. Schudson, *Discovering the News*, 178, 187.

32. Marc Weingarten, *The Gang That Wouldn't Write Straight* (New York: Crown Publishers, 2006), 6.

33. Wolfe, *The New Journalism*, 46, 48.

34. Weingarten, *The Gang That Wouldn't Write Straight*, 124.

35. Norman Mailer, *The Armies of the Night: History As a Novel, The Novel as History* (New York: Plume, 1994), 255.

36. Alfred Kazin, "The Trouble He's Seen: *The Armies of the Night* by Norman Mailer," *New York Times*, May 5, 1968.

37. Kazin, "The Trouble He's Seen."

38. Michiko Kakutani, "Mailer Talking," *New York Times*, June 6, 1982, 3(7).

39. Weingarten, *The Gang That Wouldn't Write Straight*, 270.

40. Kakutani, "Mailer Talking," 3(7).

41. Stephen Colbert, *The Colbert Report*, Comedy Central, October 17, 2005.

42. Andrew Sullivan, "Why I Blog," *Atlantic* (November 2008).

43. Peter J. Boyer, "One Angry Man," *New Yorker*, June 23, 2008.

44. Kersti Yllo, "Political and Methodological Debates in Wife Abuse Research," in *Feminist Perspectives on Wife Abuse*, ed. Kersti Yllo and Michele Bograd (Newbury Park, Calif: Sage Publications, Inc., 1988), 48.

45. Brent Cunningham, "Toward a New Ideal: Re-thinking Objectivity in a World of Spin," *Columbia Journalism Review* (July/August 2003).

46. Mindich, *Just the Facts*, 142.

3

✎

From the Heart

The Benefits of Being Emotionally Invested

Former *Houston Chronicle* reporter Daniel Vargas grew up a witness to violence. His oldest sister was a victim of her husband's abuse. In 2001, something inside Vargas clicked when he heard about Angela Hudson, a mother of five whose estranged husband had deliberately set her on fire. Angela and Keeper Ray Hudson had been arguing the night before, and Keeper had shown up the next morning carrying a duffel bag. Inside were a knife and a jug of gasoline. Threatening to stab her if she didn't hold still, Keeper bound Angela's wrists and ankles with clothesline wire, doused her chest with the gas, and threw a lit match. By the time police and firefighters arrived, Angela was severely burned from her head to her waist. Her ears had been singed to their auditory canals.

When Vargas first read a newspaper brief about Angela, he says he was "instantly drawn to the story." It was "partly because of the brutality of the assault. Mostly because it hit a nerve."[1] Vargas tells me, "My mind was just attuned to these types of stories. At the time I heard about it, memories and images didn't rush into my mind, but past experiences had molded my psyche, so I was aware of this story's importance." In the nine months that he followed Hudson and her family through her painful recovery, Vargas connected with the story on a personal level. In his twelve-part series, he wrote about Hudson's ordeal with a kind of tenderness rarely seen in daily newspaper writing. In this scene, he described her injuries just after the incident:

Angela Hudson's head is swollen, and a machine pumps life into her lungs. Netting holds bandages wrapped around her face and neck, leaving only her

33

eyes and badly scarred lips visible. Once she favored [her mother Doris] Tate so much that strangers assumed they were sisters. "When I see her face, my heart melts," Tate says. "It takes every ounce of energy to keep from breaking down and screaming and getting out all the anger."[2]

When Vargas received an award for his series, he revealed his own experiences with violence to his audience:

> Like many others, I grew up a witness to domestic violence, although less violent in comparison to Hudson's situation. Yet, the memories of that day are vivid. I can still hear the squeal of police sirens. I can still see my older sister (time and time again) black and blue after her husband beat her. I can still smell the fear. I knew firsthand that the effects go beyond the offender and victim. They extend generations. When I approached Hudson's mother, Doris Tate, in the burn unit waiting room, I recognized her face. It was one of loneliness and heartache. I had seen that face before.[3]

Vargas's personal history allowed him to connect with the story on a more emotional level, and the result was a dramatic shift in how he told the story. Rather than concentrating on the mechanics of the crime and "why" it was committed (as if there could be a legitimate reason for such brutality), he described the violence from the perspective of Hudson and her family. Vargas was not a distant observer but a compassionate, feeling participant. He did not close himself off from Hudson's pain—or from his own painful memories—but used these emotions to inform his work. "I didn't just sympathize," says Vargas. "I empathized, and that made me a better reporter."

In her book *Emotionally Involved: The Impact of Researching Rape*, Rebecca Campbell laments the fact that, in her field, rape is often defined in cold legal or clinical terms—terms that lack "the voice of the victim, the feelings of the victim, the emotions of surviving rape." While she understands this may be part of researchers' attempts to appear "unbiased and rigorous," she fears that, without the emotional dimension, the research on rape may not be accurate or complete. "Just how good is our science if it is not known from the experience of the rape survivor?" Campbell asks. "How good is our research if we maintain, however explicitly or implicitly, that rape can be about logic, intellect, and objectivity, when it seems to be about emotion?"[4]

Like Campbell, many of the journalists I interviewed said that to deny their emotions around violence was to deny the most vital part of the story. "Often, in the case of tragedy especially, emotion is in fact the story," says Jim Willis, who covered the Oklahoma City bombing. "If what you are covering are people in crisis—especially reacting to a crisis that has occurred—you are covering emotions. So to ignore those emotions or to not use storytelling methods that convey accurately those (and only those) emotions is tantamount to missing the point of the story in the first place."

No doubt, feeling the pain of violence has its emotional risks, but most of the journalists I interviewed were grateful for the insights—into their subjects, their audiences, and ultimately themselves—those painful experiences provided. Miles Moffeit, the reporter for the *Denver Post* who co-wrote the series on rape in the military, recalls the day he met one of his sources at a restaurant in Washington, D.C. While serving in the army, the woman had been raped twice by fellow officers. Clutching her dog tags, she recounted the most brutal details of her assaults and how the military had tried to cover them up. "I'm a soldier, and what they did was betray me," she told Moffeit. "But I want to tell my story, so I can be a soldier and help other women in the Army." Moffeit listened for five hours as the woman read from her diary, her hands shaking as she turned the pages. He was furious with the military for what they'd done to her. But rather than squelch his emotions, Moffeit dug deeper. "Once you feel someone's pain, you get angry, and that emboldens you to tell their story," he says. "A stoic person can't do these stories."

LEARNING TO CARE ABOUT OUR SUBJECTS

In addition to wanting to understand their stories in a more profound way, many of the journalists I interviewed said they were tired of hiding behind their notebooks and video cameras—"capturing" the words of their interviewees but never really connecting with these people on a human level. They were tired of putting their stories first and their subjects' needs last—a hierarchy that often caused pain or shame for the people they covered. In *Dispatches from the Edge*, Cooper addresses this issue when he describes his decision to not wear a bulletproof vest anymore during the war in Bosnia in 1993.

> Surrounded by Bosnians who didn't have protection, I felt that it was inappropriate for me to stay sealed off. I wanted them to tell me their stories, risk exposing themselves to me. I couldn't ask that of someone if I wasn't willing to expose myself as well. Without the vest, I could feel the breeze on my chest, the closeness of another person, the sense of loss in everyone's embrace.[5]

Like Ed Murrow's decision to travel through London in an open car during World War II, Cooper no longer wanted to be seen as an outsider—above the human fray and more deserving of protection than the people he covered. This allowed him to form more intimate relationships with his subjects.

As I came to realize in my own career, when I ignored my feelings in covering violence, I, too, never really "saw" my subjects on anything but a superficial level. I recorded their interviews, wrote up my notes, and thought I'd captured "the truth" in my ratio of the "pro versus con" people with whom I spoke. But my emotional absence during this process makes my stories seem vacant and drifting. It was only when I was older—and confident enough to question what I'd been taught—that I realized that I could not write truthfully about people unless I was willing to "know" them on a more personal level.

In *Social Science and the Self*, Susan Krieger talks about how, during interviews with her research subjects, she felt like she had to disappear or risk "entering into very messy relationships, unclear relationships, in which I would have needs." And those needs, she worried, would never be met—or, if they were, she feared it would be inappropriate. Because of her concerns, Krieger adopted what she describes as a "very alienated and painful strategy of interviewing" in which she denied herself as part of the equation. Ultimately, this made her resentful toward her interview subjects—a feeling that was bound to impact her work. "Sitting and talking with someone else about her life, when I deny myself, I feel, all the while, that she is denying me," she says. What's more, Krieger's self-denials made it "much harder for me to understand anything or anyone," she says, because she wasn't allowed to experience her subjects or research except in the abstract.[6]

"To create change, you have to tell human stories. That means building relationships with our subjects as real people," says Moffeit. "That's so counter to objective journalism, but we shouldn't shy away from relationships that help us understand." While writing his series on rape in the military, Moffeit developed a close relationship with one of his subjects. A former Marine, Sally Fictum was raped by a fellow soldier at the age of nineteen. After filing a complaint with the military, she was investigated for lying and, she says, humiliated by her commanders. Given what she had endured, Moffeit handled their relationship with care. He knew that personal boundaries were important, although he admits he redrew those boundaries often, depending on the circumstances. "It's a real dance," he says. "She was dealing with myriad problems and was reluctant to seek long-term counseling. I didn't want to be in a position of power and give her any kind of advice." Still, Moffeit says, he and Fictum did manage to connect on a deeper level. And he knows that if he hadn't waded into the risky waters of human relationships, he never would have understood the story on anything but a superficial level. In dissolving the line between the reporter and the reported, he gained Fictum's trust—and powerful insight into what she'd endured. "If you don't get that close to someone, you don't understand the emotional truth of what's happening to them," he says.

Of course, with this more emotionally engaged style comes a greater awareness of a subject's needs and vulnerabilities, which I would argue is another benefit of this more compassionate approach to journalism. When an interviewee becomes a human first and a source second, journalists often must balance the need to "get the story" with a personal concern for their subject. An interviewee is not merely a source of information or the center of a good yarn but a person who deserves respect and consideration. This can be the case for social scientists who take a more emotional approach to their work as well. "Caring means thinking through what people will get out of participating in the research process, what they would gain, and what effect it would have on their lives," says Campbell. This means balancing "the requirements of science with a personal concern for the well-being of those impacted by a project," she says.[7]

Campbell, for instance, believes that researchers should not automatically share all of their findings with the rest of the world. Instead, they might consider holding back details that could harm their subjects. She says the notion of releasing all information "in the best interest of science" is too simplistic. Being emotionally connected to your topic means looking at it from other points of view, including those of your participants.[8]

Up until recently, the notion that journalists owed something to their subjects would have been considered near blasphemy among America's news media. In his 1973 anthology of New Journalism, Tom Wolfe said that reporters who developed a personal relationship with their subjects and then became "stricken with a sense of guilt, responsibility, obligation" were asking for trouble. Inevitably, these journalists produced "second-rate work, biased in such banal ways that they embarrass even the subjects they think they are 'protecting,'" he said. Wolfe maintained that journalists shouldn't compromise their stories for anyone. Indeed, he said, if a journalist "doesn't believe that his own writing is one of the most important activities going on in contemporary civilization, then he ought to move on to something else that he thinks is."[9]

Thanks to organizations like the Dart Center for Journalism & Trauma, this idea of journalism's moral superiority (which, in turn, allows reporters to act with impunity) is starting to shift. Based out of Columbia University's Graduate School of Journalism in New York City, Dart seeks to teach journalists how to be sensitive to crime victims' needs and not retraumatize them with overly aggressive or insensitive reporting. Dart encourages journalists to be mindful of what they put in print, to perhaps avoid using unnecessarily gory details or images from a crime, and to not hound the victims or their families for interviews.

Being sensitive to crime victims is a lesson that Laura Sullivan, a correspondent for National Public Radio, took to heart in her 2007 report on the sexual abuse of Native American women. Sullivan interviewed at least a dozen people on a reservation in the Dakotas—rape counselors, victims, doctors, and so forth—who were either raped themselves or knew women who were. The women's assailants were never charged because few tribes have the money to police their own lands. Sullivan tells me she felt an enormous debt to the women who shared their stories with her.

"There's so much responsibility in terms of what to do with that material and how to portray them in a way that they feel comfortable with so that they won't, God forbid, be retraumatized," she says. Rather than simply include these women's stories to pump up the drama of her report, Sullivan made sure they served a purpose. "I want to make sure this person's personal tragedy I'm including is going to further the message of my story and isn't just in there because it's salacious or because you feel like you need to include a horrible tragedy," she explains. "It's making a point in the story that, without it, that point would be lost."

The Dart Center also encourages reporters to give survivors of violence some sense of control over a story. For instance, Dart advises letting interviewees set some of the conditions of an interview—to state whether they'd like to sit or stand, for instance, and to ask any questions they might have beforehand. Daniel Vargas even went so far as to tell Angela Hudson's mother that he would stop the story at any point, particularly if Hudson decided she didn't want it told once she was well enough to be informed of the series. "You're dealing with a family that had no feeling of control," Vargas says, and he sensed from his own experiences that "they needed some control."

Victim empowerment is an issue near and dear to Bruce Shapiro, Dart's executive director and a survivor of violence himself. On a warm summer evening in 1994, Shapiro was out for coffee with two friends in New Haven, Connecticut, when a man named Daniel Silva stormed into the coffeehouse with a hunting knife. In the midst of a psychotic episode, Silva went on a stabbing spree, severely wounding Shapiro and several others. Recovering from his physical wounds was difficult enough, but Shapiro's emotional trauma was compounded by the local media's insensitive ways.

Shapiro was just hours out of surgery, and reporters were calling his hospital room. Even worse, a local paper ran what he once described as "spectacularly distressing full-color photos of the crime scene complete with the coffee bar's bloody windowsill." As Shapiro learned, when the news media's main concern is getting the story rather than treating their subjects with care, they can aggravate an already acute sense of helplessness among crime victims. "To the victim of a violent crime the press may reinforce the perception that the world is an uncomprehending and dangerous place," Shapiro wrote in an article for the *Nation*. However, if the press is sensitive to the needs of trauma survivors, it can have the opposite effect: "Sensitive reporting can for the crime victim be a kind of ratification of the seriousness of an assault, a reflection of the community's concern."[10] And that sense of concern can help survivors begin to heal from the devastating traumas they've experienced.

HELPING AUDIENCES BREAK THE CYCLE OF VIOLENCE

Sensitive reporting also can help audiences view violence in a different light—as the serious and painful problem it is rather than as a source of entertainment. Lately, much has been made of the notion of "compassion fatigue" in the United States—how Americans have lost their compassion for those who are suffering and view violence and tragedy only through the sensational prism of crime shows and the evening news. It's as if, for most of us, watching crime on TV or reading about it in the paper is like an out-of-body experience—we watch ourselves watching it but don't really register the brutality of what we are seeing. Instead, we are almost lulled by these tragic images. They seem to offer comfort rather than *discomfort*—at least we're safe in our own homes, we tell ourselves.

I maintain that journalists must learn to care about their stories first before they ever can expect audiences to. Only when they connect with violence on a personal level—only when they allow themselves to feel the anguish of what it's like to be the victim of a crime—will we inspire readers and viewers to "think" about violence differently, and to act. "If we can report on violence, victimization, and loss in a way that allows the third party, the reader, to take it in and if the larger context is available, we may not be as likely to respond with cruelty," says Frank Ochberg, who founded the Dart Center in 1999. By cruelty, he means, "enjoying or being indifferent to" the suffering of another. For Ochberg, reversing this human tendency is the first step in getting at the roots of why we live in such a violent society.

In an article published on the website of Gift From Within, an international nonprofit for survivors of trauma and violence, Ochberg notes that we have been "programmed" since childhood to seek out disturbing stories as a way to safely process them from a distance. "Fairy tales tell of children stuffed in ovens, ogres who snatch babies from princesses, giants who eat boys and girls," he says. "Our early encounters with fictional horror are arousing but safe and entertaining . . . We take in pictures of predators and predation, of monsters and mayhem, so that we have templates in the brain when real danger strikes."[11]

But according to Gina Ross, founder and president of the International Trauma-Healing Institute in Los Angeles, we have become addicted to these horrific stories as we experience them over and over again—"simultaneously mesmerized and anesthetized by violence and tragedy." As a result, we have become caught in what Ross describes as a "secondhand trauma vortex"—"a whirlpool of overstimulation" in which our capacity to "think and reflect, to empathize and take action" has been compromised.[12]

Unfortunately, the majority of news media feed this vortex by endlessly publishing what Ochberg calls Act One stories about violence. In these, journalists describe the violence in sensational ways that create arousal and interest among audiences—a kind of "paradoxical pleasure" that makes us feel safe. Ochberg compares Act One stories to the "if it bleeds, it leads" mentality of some newsrooms. "The TV news reports that show crime scenes and ambulances—hot images rather than cool commentary—are expectable subjects at six o'clock," he says.

To break this hypnotic pull of violence, Ochberg encourages journalists to move beyond the first act of trauma news. In his view, there are two other acts to consider, each having its own critical role in how we perceive and respond to violence. In Act Two, reporters are a bit more emotionally aware, and they tend to focus more on the victim's recovery process than on the traumatic event itself. "Act Two, well told, includes all of the stages of trauma and recovery," says Ochberg. It operates like a classical tragedy in that "a person reflects upon loss but is thankful for friends. Spiritual themes emerge. The survivor considers the meaning of life." Ochberg does not consider Act Two stories to be superior to or more important than Act One stories. They both serve a purpose, he says. The problem is that while Act One stories are splashed all over the front page and evening news, Act Two stories are often "buried in the features section, or relegated to a TV magazine." As a result, Act Two's message of hope and resilience—and, thus, its potential to help break the repetitive cycles of violence—is often lost.

In Ochberg's final act of trauma news, there is no silver lining to the violence like in Act Two. Act Three stories also offer no "paradoxical pleasure" or excitement for the reader or viewer, as in Act One. Instead, stories in this third act bring out negative emotions—in the journalist and in his or her audience—with very little compensating positive emotion. They are the stories we hate to hear—like the massacres in Rwanda and Sierra Leone. "You won't get anything out of it that pleases you or makes you want more," Ochberg tells me.

As journalists, we have a responsibility to write these Act Three stories and to not spin them into Act Twos, says Ochberg. If we don't—and we try to ease our audience's discomfort with a phony sense of resolution or redemption—we will not convey the sheer horror of some types of trauma. No doubt, this more realistic and nuanced approach to violence encompassed in acts two and three will have its emotional costs—for the news media and society—but ultimately, moving beyond the first act of trauma is the only way to interrupt the mesmerizing effect of violence on society. It is the only way to help people "see" violence for what it is—not as a source of pleasure or "better him/her than me" satisfaction but as an epidemic that effects all of us and must be addressed.[13]

UNDERSTANDING OUR OWN REACTIONS TO VIOLENCE

A more emotional approach to violence can benefit individual journalists as well. Research suggests that among certain professionals—especially those who deal with sensitive and emotionally disturbing issues—being more aware of one's feelings can result in a stronger sense of self and more satisfying personal relationships outside the workplace. On a professional level, reporters who are more in tune with their emotions during violent events also may be able to manage their feelings better and avoid having them dominate the thinking and feeling process. In addition, reporters who acknowledge their feelings around the emotionally challenging topic of violence may be less prone to psychological problems—an issue I will explore in greater detail in chapter 5.

To examine the potential effects a more emotionally engaged approach might have on a reporter's personal life, I reviewed studies that examined the role of feelings (or the lack of them) in other professions with similar emotional challenges. In one, researchers followed students during their first three years of training at a major medical school in the Southwest. Like journalists, the medical students had been taught that their feelings—particularly uncomfortable ones around the human body—should remain private, so the students developed a variety of ways to dull their emotional responses on the job. Some students feared that this "desensitization" process was spilling over into their personal lives. "Quietly, because their concern is private and therefore uncertain, students ask questions we might all ask," say the study's authors. "Will we lose our sensitivity to those we serve? To others in our lives? To ourselves? Will we even know it is happening?"[14]

As in the news profession, the methods students used to deny their emotions included maintaining an intellectual distance from their work and employing a kind of gallows humor as a way to relieve tension. This "depersonalization" of something so personal to them left some of the students with a "vague and unsettling sense of loss," say the researchers. One first-year female student had this to say about a cadaver she had worked on:

The heart. I know it's just a blood pump. Mostly muscle. Valves. But it's something more, too. Interesting to touch it, see it. But it felt funny. Like (pause) I went up in my head when we lifted out his heart. Funny feeling (pause) partly physical.

Some of the students felt a sense of self-estrangement as they were forced to deny any personal meaning to their work. Others carried this more distant and clinical perspective home with them and feared it was interfering with their ability to be intimate with a partner. As one male student told the researchers:

In GYN you don't think so much in sexual terms. Not with that big piece of metal (the speculum) in her. But there's no metal at home, and I still don't feel the same about it. They say you get over this pretty quick. I wonder how. What will it be like later?[15]

While I did not find studies on this issue specifically related to the news media, as a journalist I certainly can relate to this struggle between the personal and professional. Intimate relationships are challenging for me, as I often find it hard to step out of my role as inquisitor and relate to people on a more personal level. When talking with loved ones, I tend to go into interviewer mode as a way to deflect attention from myself. During times of stress or sadness, I have noticed that accessing my emotions can be difficult. I am usually a character in my own story rather than a human being experiencing something painful.

It's hard to say whether journalism contributed to this tendency of mine to remain aloof and disengaged—or whether I was drawn to journalism because of it. I think that is the case for many reporters. For some, past experiences of abuse or other types of trauma have dulled their emotional responses to violence—have taught them that it is safer to operate on a kind of emotional autopilot than to experience that kind of pain all over again. For others, experiences in the field have made them numb overall. I can say that since I began to view my role as a journalist differently and to feel more, my personal life has become more emotional—more "truthful"—as well.

Very gradually I am starting to allow myself to be more vulnerable, to let in people and emotions in ways I didn't before. I have learned that when I work through my feelings—no matter how ugly or painful they might be—I can be more present, more alive as a journalist and a human being. I also have realized that when I feel another person's anguish—or my own—I have more empathy, and this makes me a better reporter, friend, and life partner.

But how much emotion is too much emotion in covering stories about violence? When do we, as journalists, swim so much in our own feelings that we lose sight of the shore—and compromise our professional duties? Ochberg, who has worked with countless journalists over the years, says it depends on the person and the situation. "A low but perceptible titter of emotion can give a writer a qualitative advantage, bringing useful images and phrases to mind," he says. "Emotion is not only quantitative, but qualitative. It helps a reporter to perceive such 'flavors' of emotion as shame, guilt, humiliation, frustration, irritation, resentment, and grief."

However, he says, there is a fine line between feeling emotions and being ruled by them. At times, our feelings can be so strong and can reach such a pitch that they interfere with the reporting process. "When the emotion of the reporter distorts recognition of the flavor of emotion in a source of a story, it is crucial that the reporter overcome that distortion," Ochberg maintains. "Accuracy is critical. The instrument of news-gathering, a reporter's keen eye, must be clear."

In *Emotionally Involved*, Campbell describes a process known as "emotion work theory" as a way for professionals to acknowledge their emotions but prevent them from interfering with their work. According to Campbell, this theory is usually referred to in the context of doctors or service workers like flight attendants and nurses—people who must attend to others' feelings. "This situational mandate to help others feel a certain way can run amok with what one actually feels," Campbell explains. For instance, a flight attendant might feel like yelling at passengers, but he or she must repress such feelings—must temper his or her emotional reaction—according to the dictates of the job. Emotion work, then, is the work of being aware of your emotions so that you can manage them.[16]

Campbell and her team engaged in emotion work throughout their project. In preparing for their interviews, she says, "we had to pull into ourselves, blocking out the rest of our lives (temporarily) so we could give a hundred percent of our attention to the rape survivor." But it was during the interview process itself that the need for emotion work was the greatest. Campbell and her colleagues had some guidelines in this respect. She says:

> As feminist interviewers, we planned on engaging our participants, sharing information and feelings. We would not sit there showing nothing, revealing nothing. If we were upset, then our project's ethic dictated that we could show those feelings. But only to a point. The interview should always be about the victim; she is the focus, not us. To gauge what we should and should not reveal, I offered this guideline in training: if you think your reaction would prompt the survivor to stop talking about what happened to her so she could attune to your feelings, that's too much emotion revealed.

Campbell says that she and her researchers never got close to the point of disrupting an interview. For the most part, they managed to control how much they revealed to their subjects. But, she says, it was hard work.[17]

When Plymouth, Massachusetts filmmaker Beth Murphy was working on a documentary about two women who had lost their husbands on September 11, she, too, walked a fine line between showing her emotions and not having them overtake the interview process. Both of her subjects had been pregnant at the time of the attack, and their husbands had perished on separate planes that had crashed into the World Trade Center. Murphy recalls when she had to ask each woman, in on-camera interviews, to recount the awful events of that day. "There were times when, during the most emotional portions of their story, they were the most stoic," says Murphy. "Those were the times I felt so overwhelmed, knowing how hard they were trying to be okay with what they were saying." At certain points during the interview, Murphy would find herself getting teary—and feeling guilty for displaying her feelings. "I never had to take time away from the interview, but I remember feeling like, 'This is the last thing they need.'"

Despite the challenges of this more emotionally engaged approach, most of the reporters I interviewed felt like their stories—and their audiences, subjects, and they themselves—had benefited from this new and deeper connection. In *Let Us Now Praise Famous Men*, James Agee talks about achieving a kind of "relative truth" in his reporting. He mentions it in relation to his subject, George Gudger, and how he, Agee, can only view Gudger through his own subjective lens. He wrote:

> I am confident of being able to get at a certain form of the truth about him, *only if* I am as faithful as possible to Gudger as I know him, to Gudger as, in his actual flesh and life (but there again always in my mind's and memory's eye) he is. But of course it will be only a relative truth.
>
> Name me one truth within human range that is not relative and I will feel a shade more apologetic of that.[18]

The reporters I interviewed had a similar philosophy. Rather than relegating their topics to a detached "voice of God" type of format, these journalists captured a more complicated type of truth—their truth. Yes, it was subjective, but as Agee noted, is there really any other kind? In taking such a risk, these reporters moved closer to my ideal of what a journalist's role should be—not as a mere stenographer but an interpreter and analyzer, someone who draws on his or her every asset to decipher the world's complexities. If we are to redefine journalism in more compassionate terms, I believe its future lies with reporters like the ones in this book. They give me hope and a reason to keep reading.

NOTES

1. Daniel Vargas, *Acceptance Speech* (given at the Dart Center for Journalism & Trauma's annual Dart Award for Excellence in Reporting on Victims of Violence ceremony, McGraw-Hill Auditorium, New York, April 2003).

2. Daniel Vargas, "Legacy of Love & Pain," *Houston Chronicle*, February 24, 2002, Lifestyles, 1.

3. Vargas, *Acceptance Speech*.

4. Rebecca Campbell, *Emotionally Involved: The Impact of Researching Rape* (New York: Routledge, 2002), 110, 116–17.

5. Anderson Cooper, *Dispatches from the Edge: A Memoir of War, Disasters, and Survival* (New York: HarperCollins, 2006), 67.

6. Susan Krieger, *Social Science and the Self: Personal Essays on an Art Form* (New Brunswick, N.J.: Rutgers University Press, 1991), 161–64.

7. Campbell, *Emotionally Involved*, 128.

8. Campbell, *Emotionally Involved*, 143.

9. Tom Wolfe, *The New Journalism* (London: Picador, 1975), 67–68.

10. Frank Ochberg, "Trauma News: Story in Three Acts," *Gift from Within*, www.giftfromwithin.org/html/threeact. html (accessed July 9, 2009).

11. Bruce Shapiro, "One Violent Crime," *Nation*, April 3, 1995, 450.

12. Gina Ross, *Beyond the Trauma Vortex: The Media's Role in Healing Fear, Terror, and Violence* (Berkeley, Calif.: North Atlantic Books, 2003), 94–96.

13. The above was gleaned from a series of interviews with Ochberg and from the *Gift From Within's* website.

14. Allen C. Smith, III and Sherryl Kleinman, "Managing Emotions in Medical School: Students' Contacts with the Living and the Dead," *Social Psychology Quarterly* 52, no. 1, Special Issue: Sentiments, Affect and Emotion (1989): 68.

15. Smith and Kleinman, "Managing Emotions in Medical School," 58–68.

16. Campbell, *Emotionally Involved*, 103.

17. Campbell, *Emotionally Involved*, 104–5.

18. James Agee, *Let Us Now Praise Famous Men* (Boston: Houghton Mifflin, 1941), 211.

4

❧

It's Personal

Gender, Medium, and More

In July 2000, documentary filmmaker Beth Murphy was teaching a journalism class at the American University of Paris. She and her students went on a field trip to Amnesty International for a lesson on genocide. As they were leaving, they walked past a room with a large cardboard box in it. "Have any of you ever seen a burqa in real life?" an Amnesty representative asked. "Have you ever tried one on?" Several at a time, Murphy and her students donned the bright blue garments, peering out at one another through the burqas' small mesh screens. "For the first time, I tried to imagine what it would be like to live behind a burqa," Murphy tells me. "That moment had a big impact on me. I knew life was horrific for women and that the Taliban laws were barbaric and extreme, but I hadn't touched it and felt it yet. That was the first moment."

Engulfed in the burqa's billowing folds, Murphy felt herself getting angry. She resonated with the plight of Afghan women, who had to cover their bodies out of fear for their lives. When Murphy finally visited Afghanistan in 2004, she was determined not to feel ashamed of her sex. "I had a sense of, 'I'm not invisible because I won't allow myself to be, even though this society wants me to be,'" she says.

Murphy was in Afghanistan to film a documentary about two American widows who'd lost their husbands in the two planes that had crashed into the World Trade Center on September 11. At the time, both women were pregnant with daughters. But rather than lash out at the people of Afghanistan, where 9/11 terrorists had been trained, Susan Retik and Patti Quigley formed a nonprofit to help Afghan war widows, with whom they felt a profound connection. As a woman herself, Murphy felt a profound connection with Quigley and Retik. "From the moment I met them both, they reminded me of either myself or my sisters in some way," says Murphy. "It was immediate. Their personalities. Little things, like humor."

Kersti Yllo, the feminist sociologist, says it's only natural for women journalists to gravitate toward issues involving other women—and feel connected to their female subjects. "Life experience shapes your perspective and your sensitivity and your openness," she explains. And when it comes to violence, women instinctively can relate to the plight of survivors. Because we live in what Rebecca Campbell describes as a rape culture that is saturated with stories about women who have been raped and brutalized, whether a woman has been victimized or not, she lives with the fear of violence much more than a man does. Female journalists, then, often have instant empathy for women victims. The anger, fear, and sadness that survivors often feel are not hard for a female reporter to access. She has experienced them on some level already just by the sheer fact of being a woman in today's society.

In this chapter, I will explore how various factors like gender, medium, ethnicity, and employment status influence this concept of emotionally engaged reporting. For instance, women are typically assigned to cover more emotional and intimate types of stories, while men tend to write about more public topics like politics and business.[1] Paradoxically, women are not allowed to be as openly emotional about their subjects as men are. Just think if a woman had been as emotional about Hurricane Katrina as Anderson Cooper was. Would she have been applauded for her courage or booed for not being tough enough? And how often do you see female news commentators express the kind of outrage that Bill O'Reilly does? Male reporters, on the other hand, often have a harder time connecting with female crime victims, whose abusers most often have been men.

And what about the videographer or photographer? Shooting violence often has a greater emotional impact on these visual journalists because they must get closer to the action in order to capture it. A print reporter can piece together his or her narrative with second-hand accounts and telephone interviews, but videographers and photographers actually must witness the violence. There is also the issue of freelancers versus staffers. Without the security of a full-time job, freelancers sometimes are more reluctant to admit to a story's emotional impact, for fear of seeming unprofessional and not getting more work.

Finally, there is the impact a medium like television can have on a journalist's ability to form an intimate relationship with his or her subject. Cameras, lights, and microphones can have a chilling effect on a subject's willingness to open up about his or her personal experiences. Certainly, they serve as more of a physical barrier between the journalist and interviewee.

GENDER AND ETHNICITY

It's hard to talk about gender in emotionally engaged reporting without getting into feminist ideology. In social science, the objective voice has been equated with the white male voice, which is still the dominant voice in society. The same could be said about journalism, a profession where men still outnumber women, especially in the top echelons. "I think white males don't understand that they're operating from a privileged place in society—the notion that their view has been equated with objectivity and that other alternative views, like those of women, are biased," says Yllo.

To shield themselves from accusations of bias, some women journalists actually will overcompensate by rigidly adhering to the objective mandate, or they will chide themselves when they do feel emotional about a story. Often, they will try to hide their feelings in the field, particularly around their male colleagues. "In my career, being a woman is seen as a liability. You're perceived as weaker," says Murphy.

In general, women seem to have permission to be more emotional than men. "Our experiences lead us to being more comfortable with our emotions," says Yllo. "No one has told us constantly, 'Don't cry. Don't be a wuss.'" However, when a woman stakes a claim in a traditionally male field like war journalism, this can change. Then she is often expected to be more "male" than her male colleagues. Hannah Allam, a bureau chief for McClatchy Newspapers, says she felt such pressure as a woman and as an Arab American covering the war in Iraq. Having spent part of her childhood in the Middle East, she often felt torn between two cultures while reporting from Baghdad. She was an American journalist covering the U.S.-led invasion, but her heart was with the Iraqi people. "Every dead child you see looks like your sister or your cousin," she explains. "Not that Western reporters are immune to suffering, but this was more personal for me." As a result, Allam says, she felt much closer to her Iraqi staff—the Baghdad bureau's translators, drivers, and stringers—than she did to her American colleagues. She tells me:

> I'd hang out with Iraqis because we have more in common. . . . I could be emotional with my Iraqi staff and then find myself being really fake with Western colleagues. There were definitely exceptions—not that they [her American colleagues] didn't feel the same pain or heartache. A lot of them lost drivers, translators, friends. But they internalized it in a different way.

In the field, Allam also felt a certain amount of pressure to squelch her feelings, even when confronted with the most horrific images. "I'd just find myself switching into objective reporter mode at a scene of a suicide bombing and reporting, 'This is a leg, this is a head, this is a pool of blood.

Is it dime-sized or quarter-sized?'" she says. And later, if she did try and discuss what she felt or saw, "there would always be those guy reporters who'd say, 'You're not going soft on me, are you?'"

Despite these pressures in the field, female war correspondents like Allam do not appear to be any more susceptible to psychological stress than their male counterparts except in one area—childbirth. In 2000, Anthony Feinstein, a neuropsychiatrist from Toronto, embarked on the first-ever study on how war journalists deal with the pressures of their profession. Most of the women correspondents he interviewed showed a "striking resilience to the emotional consequences of trauma," except when they became pregnant and gave birth. In that instance, women who seemed to have survived their wartime experiences unscathed suddenly started showing signs of psychological stress, often battling intrusive thoughts and anxiety. "Becoming a parent and bonding intensely with your newborn awakens strong protective instincts," Feinstein explains in his book *Dangerous Lives: War and the Men and Women Who Report It*. "It also sensitizes you to the grief of those who have lost children in conflict."[2] Feinstein's findings were borne out in my own research.

After producing *Beyond Belief*, Beth Murphy became pregnant with a daughter of her own. This connected the Massachusetts filmmaker to the two widows' plight in a way she hadn't been before. After her daughter, Isabelle, was born, Murphy also found herself thinking about the widows of Afghanistan she'd met and their children. She tells me:

> I can't imagine what it might be like to be a woman in Afghanistan, to be totally impoverished. Your husband beats you. Your children are neglected. It just makes me so sad. And being able to visualize the women who are so poor and have so few resources and have society tell you you're nothing and to know who those women are, it feels like a heavy weight.
>
> Since Isabelle was born, I think about the child component even more. I can't imagine someone harming a child or yelling at a child. So the idea that women around the world are forced to make decisions about kids they don't want to make or forced to think about leaving their kids to have any sort of financially stable life, it kills me. There are times when I wish I could turn my brain off.

For other female reporters, becoming pregnant and having a child sensitized them to violence in more general ways.

"Maybe it's having something that is so helpless," says NPR reporter Laura Sullivan, who was pregnant at the time of her report on the sexual abuse of Native American women. "There's this sort of instinct—you see that helplessness in others that you didn't before. That makes these stories much more personal." For Sullivan, her pregnancy also created a sense of intimacy with the Native American women she interviewed. After all, motherhood is a bond many women share. It transcends external differences like class, ethnicity, and education. "Being pregnant made me more than just a reporter," says Sullivan. "I was a person. I was having a child. A lot of these women were mothers. . . . There was a great respect for motherhood, and mothers and children. Everybody wanted to talk about it. It was a great opening."

Obviously, not all survivors of violence are women, and there are males, like former *Houston Chronicle* reporter Daniel Vargas, who are intimately familiar with its consequences. But because women are more vulnerable to crimes like rape, they can more easily identify with the emotions of it. With sexual assault, the majority of its perpetrators are also men, which can put male reporters in an awkward position when covering sex crimes. Miles Moffeit, who co-wrote the series on rape in the military for the *Denver Post*, says that, at first, he felt uncomfortable interviewing his female subjects. These women soldiers "didn't trust men," he says. "It was awkward being a man and knowing the brutality caused by other men—that I was a symbol of that."

Bruce Lundeen, a documentary videographer, says his gender has worked both for and against him at times. As an example, he mentions a shoot in Bangladesh for which his female director wanted to interview sex workers. Lundeen felt she would have an easier time doing so without his male presence, so he sent in another woman to do the camera work. "But then there was the time we were in Pakistan, and I had to put the microphone on some of the men because they couldn't be touched by a woman, although we had a woman sound person," he says.

In general, Lundeen is a strong advocate of opening up the traditionally male venue of videography to women and other minorities. He says:

> I am definitely a proponent of getting people who don't look like me to be in the industry, because I'm a representative of the dominant culture—white male. So to be able to get other people into the industry is really important. The viewpoints are really important. I'm six feet tall. People who are five-foot-five have a different perspective. The media that we ingest is produced by the dominant culture, and we take it as universal.

But the task for women who do make it into such male-dominated fields as videography and war reporting is to not then buy into that dominant culture. If women do tend to feel more comfortable with their feelings, they could be a powerful force among the American news media, getting their peers to open up more about the emotional toll of covering violence. By tapping into their emotions and personal experiences, women journalists also have the potential to convey, on a very profound level, the depth of a survivor's tragedy.

When Murphy's documentary premiered at the Tribeca Film Festival, for instance, audiences openly sobbed during Quigley and Retik's emotional tale of grief and recovery. Murphy managed to capture the complexity of the women's feelings—the moments of joy amidst the endless bouts of grief, the guilt in moving on with their lives, and the agony and triumph of meeting Afghan widows with stories similar to (and, in many cases, even more tragic than) their own.

As I mentioned in chapter 3, until journalists learn to care about their stories, they will have a harder time getting their audiences to care. Women should be encouraged to embrace their gender rather than hide its attributes behind an objective façade. "Empathy, fortunately for us all, is not beyond human capacity; good journalism often is the means by which empathy is evoked," says Michael Schudson in his book *The Power of News*. "But who writes the story matters. When minorities and women and people who have known poverty or misfortune first-hand are authors of news as well as its readers, the social world represented in the news expands and changes."[3]

MEDIUM

When videotaping a documentary, Lundeen considers himself a "non-speaking participant" in the process. As a camera operator, he is not the one asking the subject questions, and he must take direction from the director or producer. On occasion this has forced Lundeen to go against his own personal ethics. "I've been in a position where I had to videotape things I didn't agree with, like when a director tells me, 'If they cry, get a close-up of a tear,'" he says. For Lundeen, pushing his lens into the face of grief can feel exploitive, but as a hired member of the crew, he often feels obligated to do as he is directed. In order to perform such uncomfortable tasks, Lundeen says he sometimes must "consciously tune out" his own emotions and stay focused on his camera work. He tells me:

> At the same time that I, as a connected listener, want to give a person some space, I'm zooming into them, so I do have to disconnect sometimes. I'm doing exactly the opposite of what I feel I should be doing. Hopefully, the end result is the video we're making has an impactful shot of this person. And if that person's story gets across, they will benefit. So that's a speed bump I have to get over.

This is a dilemma many videograpahers and photographers face—the impulse to act on emotions versus the professional mandate to remain focused on the technical side of their craft.

In a 2004 article in *Columbia Journalism Review*, Judith Matloff contends that because of this conflict between thinking and feeling, photographers are more susceptible to emotional stress than print reporters. "Because photographers have to get close to capture their subjects, they must switch off their human instinct to help, and this can cause inner conflict," says Matloff.[4] Many videographers and photographers also don't have control over how their images will be used, which can make the decision of whether or not to shoot something a weighty one indeed.

In the past, Lundeen has struggled with whether or not to turn off his camera—or to even go back and rewind the tape—when subjects reveal damaging information about themselves. But other videographers feel the opposite—that they are there to shoot whatever is in front of them and that it's up to their editors to then decide what to do with the footage. Kevin Burke is a cameraperson based in Baghdad, shooting the war for NBC. He has videotaped people getting shot and killed and says he does not have a problem doing so. He tells me:

> I would say that the best way to depict the wider conflict is through the experience of the individuals caught in the middle of it. Sometimes this involves seeing the lethal costs of war up close. To us, it's an important part of the story and one that the audience should be more familiar with. I am committed to bringing the reality that happens before me to our audience.

Burke says he is not there to make judgments but simply to portray war as it really is. After that, it's up to his editors to decide what to do with those images.

This process of capturing images and then letting someone else make a story out of them can leave visual journalists without a sense of closure, according to Matloff. While print reporters craft a beginning and an end to their articles, visual journalists deal more with fragments of a story.[5] And these fragments, or images, can pop up again and again for them—in their minds, on television, and in the papers—and constantly remind them of the original trauma they witnessed. "Every time you see the picture, whether it be on the front page of the newspaper or displayed for an award, you relive the sights, sounds, smells, and the adrenaline that is associated with the picture," says David Handschuh, the New York photojournalist who nearly lost his life on September 11. Lundeen agrees. "When I see pictures, no matter how much they've been cut up in editing, the whole experience comes back to me, even what we had for lunch that day," he says.

Those who are involved editing the video experience it a bit differently. Sullivan, the NPR reporter, edits with sound rather than images, but her process is similar to that of a video editor. "The first couple of times you're playing it and hearing it, you feel choked up," she says. "But then in editing you start seeing it in a very antiseptic sort of way—the pacing, etc. On the other hand, you become so familiar with the script, it's permanently etched in your head forever. It's not just text. You can hear their voices over and over again. And when you finish the story and it airs, it creeps back on you."

With her documentary *Beyond Belief*, Murphy also had a hand in the editing process. Seeing the images over and over again, she went through stages in which she felt numb to their emotional impact. "You start to wonder, 'Is anyone going to think this is powerful?'" she says. "We had no perspective." But after Murphy finished editing the documentary and let it sit for a while, she began to feel its power. Now when she watches it, "I get emotional at different times throughout the film because I relate to it differently on different days," she says. "I relate to it differently now that I have a child. How on earth could you lose your husband while you're pregnant?"

Another difference between visual/sound journalists and print reporters is equipment. In print, a notebook, pen, and possibly tape recorder are the usual tools of the trade, but in TV and radio, the logistics of covering a story are more complicated. Not only do you need more equipment like microphones, recorders, lights, and cameras but, especially in television, you need people to operate this equipment. This can add to the already artificial sense of the interview. As Campbell writes of the interview process in social science:

> In a manufactured setting, two strangers (usually) come together and one shares with the other some personal, perhaps painful, aspect of her life. . . . the interview is typically a temporary relationship, created and dissolved within mere hours. That anything real, binding, and connecting comes through is somewhat surprising.[6]

In broadcast journalism, the additional burden of the equipment can add to the strangeness of it all, the lights and camera creating the effect of a Hollywood movie set. To minimize this effect, Lundeen says he tries to get to know someone before he barges into his or her home with his camera. He wants to be as non-threatening a presence as possible. "My first inclination in a situation is to let the subjects get used to me," he says. "I don't come in and sit down and start videotaping right away. If it's a room full of people, I'll come in and sit in the middle of the room and hang."

Sullivan says it's important not to let the equipment become the "third person" in the room. "Television reporters do this very aggressive microphone work," she says. "They use these mics with big placards." But Sullivan tries her best to ignore the equipment used in her interviews and to stay focused on her subjects' words. In these face-to-face encounters, she says, it is also important to be genuine in your reactions. Sullivan tells me:

I want to know how and what they're feeling, so I can do the greatest justice to their story. And the only way I can do that is by being human, which means showing them that, yes, I think it's horrible what they've been through and, yes, I'm glad they're standing up for themselves. You reflect the emotion that they're feeling. I don't think journalists should be apologizing for this. We should be seeing people as humans so we can accurately portray them.

Sullivan's other rule is to never break eye contact with someone who is revealing something personal, particularly when it involves violence. She says:

Always make eye contact, especially if you get to the part where it's really bad. Don't break eye contact. I don't know why I feel so strongly about that. People are reading your body language. Don't blink when they get to the part where they say, "Could I have stopped it? Could I have done something?"

In this way, Sullivan conveys that she can be trusted— that she knows their personal experiences are sacred and need to be treated that way.

In terms of creating emotionally powerful stories, Sullivan feels she is at an advantage in radio. Listeners get to hear the anguish and elation in the voices of her subjects. "You can hear them if they catch their breath," she says. "You can hear sometimes the cathartic release in telling the story." Equally important, her subjects can feel a sense of empowerment—the story is being told with their own words. Sullivan also reveals emotion through her own narration. "I feel like I reveal emotion, because how can you not? This is not a police interrogation," she says.

The barrier of equipment is a dilemma I have faced as a documentary filmmaker as well. To create a sense of intimacy during videotaped interviews, I try to sit as close as possible to my subjects so that we see each other as ordinary people—not actors under hot lights, playing the roles of journalist and subject. I also will sacrifice aesthetics for comfort if I have to. If the lights are shining in an interviewee's face and distracting him or her, I'll turn them off, even if that compromises the video's quality. During the interview itself, I am like Sullivan in that I rate eye contact as the most important part of the process. I want them to see that I empathize with them—that I am listening and not just recording what they are saying.

To dismantle the hierarchy between interviewer and interviewee, I also never place my questions on a piece of paper in front of me. To me, this would signal that I knew something my subject didn't—that I was essentially dictating the course of the interview. Instead, I review my questions the night before and then allow the interviewee to steer our talk as much as I do, making it seem like less of an interrogation and more of a conversation. At the end of every interview, I ask my subject if I have forgotten anything or if they'd like to add something. In this way, I give them the final word, as is their due.

EMPLOYMENT STATUS

Being a freelance journalist, particularly one who covers war, can be one of the most stressful jobs in the industry. Freelancers often do not have the same built-in support network that staffers do. As a result, they can have a harder time processing their feelings, isolated, as they are, from their peers and anyone who possibly could help. Tina Carr is director of the Rory Peck Trust, a UK-based nonprofit that supports freelancers world-wide. She is most concerned about the fact that, unlike staffers, freelancers returning from war zones are not offered therapy or counseling sessions by the institutions for which they work. She tells me:

> With staff cameramen and reporters, when they return from conflict, there is some kind of setup to offer support if they need it. So, for example, the BBC. They're very geared up to offer psychological counseling when their people return. It's as important as a physical checkup. Freelancers don't have that. As one freelancer said to me, "It's a luxury we can't afford. We're too busy looking for the next job."

But even if freelancers were offered counseling services, they might not take advantage of them. Without the safety net of full-time work, these reporters could be more reluctant to admit to the emotional consequences of their jobs. "Professionally, they're frightened that they won't be given more work," says Carr. "I do know a woman freelance journalist who suffered from very severe PTSD [post-traumatic stress] and was quite open about it. She didn't work for four years."

The lack of counseling services (and freelancers' potential reluctance to use them) is unfortunate, considering that these journalists tend to be very personally involved in their stories. Unlike staffers, who often are assigned stories, freelancers pick their topics based on personal interest. They are paid little and often put themselves in harm's way for their stories. As a result, they can be fiercely passionate about them. In *Dangerous Lives*, Feinstein summarizes the experience of freelancers. He writes:

> Unlike agency journalists, freelancers lack support and backup should they get into difficulties, which they often can't avoid, given the nature of their work and the places visited. The benefits of working for a news agency, such as life insurance, armored vehicles for transport in and out of areas of conflict and help on the other end of a telephone line, are eschewed in favor

of independence, the choice of deciding what to do, where to go and what to record, unfettered by the constraints of the news bosses and an imposed political agenda.[7]

Free to report a story as they see fit, freelancers often are less afraid to throw off the "voice of God" type of reporting for something more personal, and they feel less pressure to achieve a kind of false objectivity by interviewing official sources only. As I mentioned in chapter 1, this can be particularly crucial in covering violence—reaching beyond official sources and the he said/she said of news for something more profound.

In his book *War Stories: The Culture of Foreign Correspondents*, anthropologist Mark Pedelty describes an underlying tension between freelancers and their full-time counterparts. His book chronicles reporters who covered El Salvador's civil war in the 1980s. The freelancers, or so-called stringers, were known as the B Team, the staffers as the A Team. Pedelty contends the stringers had several gripes with staffers. One was that these full-timers were "both physically and culturally removed from Salvadoran society." A second was that they relied "much too heavily upon elite, propagandistic sources—especially U.S. State Department officials" and were, in turn, "treated preferentially by them."[8] Freelancers, on the other hand, usually are not so removed from the societies they cover. Instead, they tend to stay longer in one location and become close to the people about whom they write. As a result, they are more emotionally impacted when these people suffer from the effects of violence or war.

There is one other emotional aspect of being a freelancer that needs to be considered—the impact such a dangerous job can have on his or her family. Stringers working in remote, war-torn regions of the world are essentially walking a tightrope without a net. As Feinstein notes, if they become injured or threatened in any way, they often have nowhere to turn. This can wreak emotional havoc on the journalist's family. "They [the families] live in a state of constant tension," says Carr. "Freelancers are going off to bear witness with no protection, no army or government behind them." To ease some of this tension, the Rory Peck Trust offers crisis support to freelancers and their families, and they also help fund hostile environment training for freelancers. These reporters, says Carr, "tend to work very much on the ground, following their noses, following a hunch. They stick around after the main news organizations leave, and they tend to work alone or with just a translator or fixer. This can expose them to danger." The Rory Peck Trust wants to ensure that these freelancers don't go into hot zones completely unprepared.

Topic, gender, ethnicity, medium, and job status are all key factors in emotionally engaged reporting. My hope is that they will be included in future discussions on the impact of violence on reporters and their stories. Each of us comes to the profession with a unique set of characteristics that allows us to connect with our topics in profound ways. While we must guard against being overwhelmed by our motives and past histories, they can guide us through the complexities of violence—and serve as valuable clues to the emotions of those who have survived it.

NOTES

1. Michael Schudson and Danielle Haas, "One of the Guys," *Columbia Journalism Review* (March/April 2008).

2. Anthony Feinstein, *Dangerous Lives: War and the Men and Women Who Report It* (Toronto: Thomas Allen Publishers, 2003), 159, 161.

3. Michael Schudson, *The Power of News* (Cambridge, Mass.: Harvard University Press, 1995), 8.

4. Judith Matloff, "Scathing Memory," *Columbia Journalism Review* (November/December 2004).

5. Matloff, "Scathing Memory."

6. Rebecca Campbell, *Emotionally Involved: The Impact of Researching Rape* (New York: Routledge, 2002), 90.

7. Feinstein, *Dangerous Lives*, 118.

8. Mark Pedelty, *War Stories: The Culture of Foreign Correspondents* (New York: Routledge, 1995), 65.

5

⌘

Feeling the Pain
The Emotional Risks of Covering Violence

Three months into her new position as Baghdad's bureau chief for McClatchy Newspapers, Hannah Allam experienced the trauma of war firsthand. In March 2004, while on vacation with her translator, she received a horrifying phone call. The night before, her translator's husband, four-year-old daughter, and mother-in-law had been murdered, execution-style. Iraqi insurgents had followed them home and opened fire on their car. Now Allam had to break the news to Ban Adil, her translator and close friend. "I got a call at eight in the morning, saying, 'They're all dead. You have to tell her,'" Allam recalls. "Having to tell my best friend that, it was awful."

When the pair returned to Baghdad, Adil's own life was threatened, and Allam knew she had to get her friend and her friend's infant son, who had not been in the car at the time of the murders, out of the country as soon as possible. The trio fled to Amman, Jordan, where they spent a month in a hotel. Allam tried to cope as best she could with a grieving widow and her crying baby. It would not be the rookie correspondent's last encounter with tragedy. Just a few months before Allam was to start a new bureau in Cairo, one of her local reporters, an Iraqi physician named Yasser Salihee, was shot to death by an American sniper. "I'd prided myself on thinking we hadn't had anyone else killed," Allam tells me. "His death, along with the callousness of the investigation, was absolutely devastating."

Allam had been just twenty-five when she'd arrived in Baghdad in July 2003. Her experiences there were a rapid initiation into the gritty world of war correspondence. Today, she still feels responsible for Salihee's death and for those of Adil's family. She wonders whether her translator's work with McClatchy was what prompted the murders. Talking on her cell phone from Baghdad, where she was covering for McClatchy's new bureau chief, Allam broke down as she talked about the tragedies she'd endured. Referring to Salihee, she said, "His poor family. I felt like I failed."

In addition to an acute sense of guilt, Allam has struggled with other symptoms of post-traumatic stress disorder (PTSD), the quintessential trauma reaction most commonly associated with soldiers returning from war. In Baghdad, she suffered from recurring nightmares and cried at odd moments—while hearing a song, for instance, or watching *The Oprah Winfrey Show*. During visits with her family in Oklahoma, she avoided seeing people and sometimes crashed from exhaustion. "The second I went on leave and got off that adrenaline high, my immune system went down," she says. "The standing joke with my mom was, 'You're coming home? Okay, I'll call the ICU and tell them to expect you.' I had stomach problems and fainting spells." Her personal life also took a hit. Allam had been engaged to be married, but hadn't been able to sustain the relationship from such a long distance and under so much stress.

Defying the stereotype of the hard-bitten conflict reporter, Allam invested her heart and soul in her stories. As a result, she was much more emotionally impacted by them. Iraq was not just another war for her—another hotspot to be chronicled. "This was my first war, and it was very personal for me," she says. "It's easier for people who have never had that attachment to just pack up and move on to Colombia or Jerusalem." But for Allam, her emotional attachment to Iraq and its people made it impossible for her to view the war dispassionately. Instead, she was consumed by the human suffering around her. "Your self is sacrificed in most cases," she says. "Now I wonder whether it was worth the emotional toll."

In *Emotionally Involved*, Rebecca Campbell says she and her research team also suffered emotionally in interviewing rape survivors. She writes:

> In varying degrees, research team members felt fear, grief, pain, and horror as the crime of rape intruded into our lives and thwarted escape. Many of us had difficulty sleeping and were haunted by nightmares in which we relived the stories of rape we heard about from the survivors. We were afraid to go out at night, and sometimes even during the day.

Such symptoms, Campbell says, are some of the consequences of caring. In allowing themselves to empathize with their subjects, she and her researchers couldn't help but experience some of their pain.[1]

Many of the journalists I interviewed agreed that when they were more personally connected to a story, they were more at risk for vicariously experiencing the intense emotions of it. While writing about Angela

Hudson's recovery from being burned alive, Daniel Vargas suffered from nightmares and often found himself on the verge of tears for no apparent reason. He became agitated and physically rundown and had flashbacks of his own sister's abuse. Kristen Lombardi also struggled with nightmares while putting together a series on clergy abuse for an alternative newspaper in Boston. "Many of my dreams had religious icons in them," she says, "and in others I was trying to protect my one-year-old niece from the Cardinal." Lombardi had grown up Catholic and had viewed priests as benevolent protectors of their flocks. Now, her research was shattering that myth, as it had for those who'd experienced the clergy abuse firsthand. "It was a big sham, and I was disgusted more than anything else," she tells me. "This was the most depraved thing you could imagine, done by people who were supposedly closest to God."

For too long the myth has prevailed that because journalists are meant to be objective, dispassionate observers, they are immune to the emotional impact of their stories. What's more, those reporters who do experience emotional or psychological stress often are so intimidated by the macho culture of the newsroom that they don't talk about their struggles. This only feeds their trauma, forcing them to "stuff" their feelings rather than express them.

While writing about Hudson, Vargas was reluctant to open up to his co-workers not only about his own experiences with violence but even about the difficulties he faced chronicling Hudson's ordeal. "Really, who wants to hear about sitting by the bedside of a burn victim? I didn't want to put this on anyone," says the former *Houston Chronicle* reporter. "Did they really want to know I saw them change her dressing and heard her screams from that? I wish I'd had someone to talk to, but my editors just wanted the facts."

Lombardi couldn't bring herself to talk about her nightmares with any of her colleagues either. "I worked in a newsroom where people were running around and talking about what President Bush had done that day," she says. "No one wanted to talk about priests molesting little boys."

According to Allam, the news media's macho culture can be even harsher for war reporters. "[T]he conflict press corps is still very much a men's club—and a white men's club, at that—and it's definitely frowned upon to 'whine' about nightmares or panic attacks," Allam tells me. "Typically, we're told to 'man up and get the job done' or 'grow some balls,' if you'll pardon the expression."

As a result of such attitudes, journalists are at least twenty years behind other so-called first responders—police officers, fire fighters, rescue workers—in dealing with the aftereffects of violence, says psychiatrist and trauma expert Frank Ochberg. He has heard the argument that, unlike police and the military, the news media can walk away from disturbing events and, thus, aren't in need of the same degree of counseling as other first responders. Ochberg disagrees. "I've had journalists say their work is more voluntary, but it's not true," he says. "Journalists can't refuse to cover car accidents, murder, and other crimes." Ochberg makes another distinction—while soldiers and police officers can help those who are suffering, reporters often feel like they can't intervene. "Journalists don't have the autonomy," he says. "They're the professional witness." This can leave them feeling helpless and exceedingly guilty for not taking action to relieve another person's suffering.

VIOLENCE AND STRESS

Of course, just because a reporter cares about his or her story and is emotionally impacted by it does not mean he or she will develop symptoms of PTSD or any other psychiatric disorder. According to Ochberg, there are many other factors involved in this equation, including how long a journalist has been covering violence. "We now know that there is a cumulative effect and journalists (especially photojournalists) are at risk as the years on the job go by," he says. "This isn't necessarily a risk for PTSD, but for depression, alcoholism, and marital strife. It is also a risk for job loss due to 'burnout' and health problems." Certain images (like the dead body of a child, for instance) or shocking events also are more likely to cause a haunting "trauma memory," says Ochberg, and result in repetitive and intrusive thoughts and memories.

Another part of the equation is the reporter him or herself. Some journalists thrive under pressure—or what Ochberg describes as a "state of arousal"—while others reach a point where the stress becomes too intense and they can no longer function. "There is an inverted U-shaped curve that biologists know correlates to arousal and performance. As stress rises, so does effective behavior—to a point," Ochberg explains. "Then stress becomes a source of interference and ability declines. Everyone's curve is different."

Ochberg suggests thinking about journalists' emotions on a scale. In the first phase, we're aware of our emotions and use them to inform our work. In the next, our emotions are so strong that they can distract us from our work. One or two steps past this, the mind and its emotions become diseased—the feelings are that intense. "There's a fork in the road, and the emotion starts to have a lot of anxiety in it," Ochberg explains. "It can become a panic disorder or something else."

Ochberg does not include PTSD on this scale of emotions because he maintains that it belongs in a different category altogether. He thinks of it not as an emotional or psychological injury but a physical one—a brain injury. "It's an injury to the function of the mind," he says. Also, Ochberg contends that other factors come into play with this disorder, including biology. "I've had my share of exposure to personal and on-the-job trauma, and I'm relatively okay," he says. "But there are some who are not, and I personally think the greatest source of the variance is genetic." Other experts in this area say that journalists who have been traumatized in the past—like those who have been sexually or physically abused as children—also are more at risk.[2]

Despite the taboo nature of the topic, research is starting to shed some light on just how many journalists may be suffering from emotional distress. Most of the research focuses on war reporters, who are relentlessly exposed to violence and some of the more shocking events and images that are likely to trigger Ochberg's so-called trauma memories. As I already have mentioned, Anthony Feinstein, a neuropsychiatrist from Toronto, is a leading expert in this area. In 2000, he conducted the first organized study on the effects of trauma and stress on war journalists. As part of his research, Feinstein collected detailed questionnaires from 140 frontline correspondents, documenting everything from their professional experience to their psychological and physical well-being. During the second phase of his study, he conducted face-to-face interviews with a random sample of twenty-eight (one in five) of these correspondents. His results confirmed just how stressful war can be for journalists.

Twenty-two percent of those he surveyed suffered from major depression—that's compared to five percent in the U.S. population at large. They also were more likely to abuse alcohol and to have suffered from failed relationships. For instance, over half of the journalists Feinstein studied were either single or divorced, compared to a control group of domestic journalists in which a third were unattached. Most disturbing, an astonishing 29 percent of the reporters surveyed suffered from PTSD, as compared to 5 percent in the general population and 7 to 13 percent among traumatized police officers. Other correspondents, while not experiencing full-blown PTSD, struggled with such debilitating symptoms as flashbacks, panic attacks, and recurring images.[3]

What is it about violence and war that can be so emotionally overwhelming for journalists? The reasons are numerous and varied. Part of it is the random nature of violence—how one person is spared while another loses his or her life. For the war correspondent specifically, the possibility of death or injury (to him or herself or a colleague) is always around the corner, and the threat is not imagined. Statistics—and such high-profile cases as the execution of *Wall Street Journal* reporter Daniel Pearl—confirm just how dangerous covering a war can be. This puts some correspondents in a constant state of panic, which can take a toll on their psyches.

In his book *Dangerous Lives: War and the Men and Women Who Report It*, Feinstein contends war journalists also deliberately seek out terrifying events and experience them over and over again. "There are always opportunities for war journalists to live willingly in cities under siege, at times subject to the same privations and dangers as the beleaguered residents—getting shot at, wounded, losing friends and colleagues," he says. "These experiences play out day after day, the weeks stretching into months and then years."[4]

A final cause of stress for those who cover violence is isolation. Conflict reporters usually work far away from loved ones, and even when they return home for a visit, they often find that friends and family can't relate to what they've gone through. Journalists who cover other forms of violence often talk of this as well—in the midst of human misery, they find it difficult to function in the ordinary outside world. "I always find myself being really self-righteous, like, 'How can the biggest decision of your day be whether you have an apple martini or a Cosmopolitan? Don't you know that people are dying?'" says Allam. "Or I'll find myself in Wal-Mart bursting into tears because there is so much decadence."

According to Feinstein, some reporters resort to alcohol as a way to "modulate their environment"—either to "relieve the mundanity of life" back home or to "blunt the fear and emotional pain" of living in a war zone.[5] "I think alcohol is the numbing drug of choice for my colleagues," Allam concurs. "I ride the elevator with them, and their breath reeks of alcohol at ten in the morning." For the conflict reporter, there are other forms of addictive relief as well, such as opium in Afghanistan and Valium in Iraq, where it can be purchased over the counter.

Allam says sexual promiscuity was another way that some of her colleagues in Iraq numbed themselves to pain—often with destructive consequences. "All the cheating that went on here—it just destroyed marriages," she says. "These are people you shared something traumatic with. There's no way people at home could relate to that."

PTSD AND THE WAR JOURNALIST

But what distinguishes this type of emotional distress from PTSD? When does psychological illness cross over into what Ochberg considers a physical illness—an illness of the brain? According to Feinstein, to suffer from PTSD, someone must have witnessed an event that involved a real or threatened death or serious injury, and his or her response to this event must involve what he identifies as the PTSD triad—intrusion, avoidance, and arousal. Intrusive symptoms include nightmares, flashbacks, and recurring images of the event, while methods of avoidance can be detachment from others or an inability to remember details of the incident. Arousal may involve hypervigilance, or a heightened sense of one's physical vulnerability, and difficulty sleeping.[6]

For Donnatella Lorch, a former *New York Times* reporter, it wasn't just images but also smells that haunted her after she covered one of the worst atrocities in human history. In the summer 2001 issue of *Media Studies Journal*, she writes about a particularly harrowing experience in Rwanda. During the genocide in 1994, she and two of her colleagues waded through the corpses of 800 men, women, and children piled up outside a church in a hamlet just east of the capital.

> We didn't talk. The smell and the stillness were too overwhelming. I'd put Vicks VapoRub on my nose and a bandanna over my mouth and tried hard to gulp little breaths. The rain had left scattered puddles, and bodies had rotted in them. It was impossible to escape that sickly, gagging stench. This place, I knew, had witnessed true evil, an evil that I could see and smell.

Today, Lorch says, "All I need is to catch a whiff of road kill" to remember that scene in Rwanda.[7]

In a recent *Columbia Journalism Review* article, Judith Matloff describes why those who experience such traumas are susceptible to post-traumatic stress. She says:

> The amygdala, an almond-shaped part of the brain that researchers believe is tied to memory, releases cascades of stress hormones such as adrenaline. Such hormones change the way the mind processes information during times of stress, lodging images like snapshots in the memory. This can contribute to post-traumatic stress disorder, when vivid recollections return well after the event, evoking the initial horror.[8]

In other words, horrifying events actually change the chemistry of the brain—and make the images all but impossible to forget. "PTSD is unfortunately a repository of horror," says Ochberg, "and it haunts and it troubles."

Post-traumatic stress has received quite a bit of attention recently, partly due to the events of September 11. As Matloff writes, "[T]he collective trauma of September 11 ushered post-traumatic stress disorder into the national lexicon."[9] However, PTSD is not a new disorder—among soldiers or war correspondents. In *Once Upon a Distant War*, William Prochnau traces the first case of PTSD among the news media to William Howard Russell, whom the British considered the first war correspondent. When Russell returned from the Crimean War in 1856, he terrified his wife with his vivid nightmares, shouting, "Tumble out! Tumble out! There's a sortie!" in the middle of the night. Ernie Pyle also "hovered near a nervous breakdown," says Prochnau, before he was killed by a Japanese sniper in 1945.[10]

More than any other war, though, Vietnam seemed to take the biggest psychic toll on journalists. Michael Herr was very open about the personal demons he battled as a result of the war. When he returned from Vietnam in 1969, he became clinically depressed and suffered what he referred to as a "massive collapse." Herr also experienced a "complete paralysis of fear," he said, which resulted in a particularly virulent case of writer's block with his book *Dispatches*. In an unpublished section of a 1976 essay for *Esquire* magazine titled "High on War," Herr talked about his inability to let go of his wartime experiences. He wrote:

> This is already a long time ago, I can remember the feelings but I can't still have them. A common prayer for the over-attached: You'll let it go sooner or later, why not do it now? Memory print, voices and faces, stories like filament through a piece of time, so attached to the experience that nothing moved and nothing went away.

According to Marc Weingarten, author of *The Gang That Wouldn't Write Straight*, Herr eventually went into psychoanalysis and battled writer's block for six years before the words finally came to him.[11]

While I use war as an extreme example, conflict reporters are not the only journalists vulnerable to emotional stress. Anyone who covers violence and other disturbing topics is at risk—some more than others, depending on their length of time in the field and their family histories. As a result, journalists who wade into the human territory of abuse and suffering must find ways to take care of themselves—and each other.

CARING FOR OURSELVES

The most important step in warding against—and healing from—harmful emotions is to acknowledge them. In other words, we need to be *more* aware of and in touch with our feelings, rather than less, in order to minimize our risk of emotional damage. That was the consensus among almost everyone I interviewed, from journalists to psychiatrists and social scientists. In order to do this, the news media need to find ways to destigmatize our emotions so that our peers won't feel forced to hide them—only to have them seep out later, in more unhealthy ways. In talking about PTSD, the worst risk factor for any journalist who covers violence, Ochberg says, "We need to establish a cadre of people who have a language for it. That will help us talk about it in more constructive ways."

For those engaged in emotionally challenging work, Campbell suggests, "creating a sense of group identity, cohesion, and support" as a preventive strategy against psychological stress. As the lead researcher of her study on rape, she found ways to make it safe for her team to be honest about their feelings. For instance, she shared her own concerns and feelings about their research as a way to "normalize" such reactions, and she conducted exit interviews to help her colleagues better process the study's impact on them. "In wrapping up a project, providing opportunities for emotional closure—a final release, reflection, integration of what has been learned and witnessed over time—are vital," she says.[12]

For the news media, the Dart Center now offers awareness and outreach programs on traumatic stress. For instance, after Hurricane Katrina, Bruce Shapiro, Dart's executive director, held a series of workshops for New Orleans' *Times-Picayune* reporters on how to handle the long-term emotional impact of the storm. "These reporters have had the same depression, post-traumatic stress, and uncertainty that everyone else in their stories experienced," says Shapiro. Part of the Dart Center's mission is to help journalists acquire emotional literacy skills—to understand the difference between depression and bereavement, for instance—as a way to process and cope with their feelings before they become debilitating. "If you want to keep your news judgment and the trust of your audience, it's very important to acknowledge how you're feeling," Shapiro contends. "A good reporter says, 'I'm angry. I don't have a house. It was destroyed. Now what can I do about it?'"

Some news organizations, particularly in broadcasting, are starting to follow Dart's lead, although critics say that, overall, the news media's efforts are not extensive enough. The BBC and CNN are often cited for their programs to help journalists cope with the aftereffects of trauma, but Feinstein says newspapers have not been as proactive in offering counseling services to their reporters. "It is fair to conclude that the majority of editors remain disturbingly unenlightened on these issues that go to the very heart of their employees' well-being," he says.[13]

But while the news media have failed to take a comprehensive, systematic approach to processing trauma, individual journalists are starting to realize the value of dealing with their feelings. Informally, they are finding ways to cope with the tragedies they witness, either through solo activities such as exercise, prayer, and poetry or by talking with each other about their shared experiences. Whenever Allam fills in for Leila Fadel, McClatchy's new bureau chief in Baghdad, she comes a few days early so that the pair, who are good friends, can "indulge in our all-night venting/crying sessions," she says. "I don't know how I could have gotten through Iraq, Beirut, Mogadishu, Tehran, etc. without her because there are precious few others in the business in whom to confide without being labeled 'too green for the job' or 'damaged goods.'"

While producing *Beyond Belief* about the two women who lost their husbands on September 11, Beth Murphy wrote poetry as a way to express
emotions that were too taboo to verbalize in her professional life. One
day, after playing with her daughter, Isabelle, Murphy imagined what
life would be like if the two of them were living in Afghanistan. In her
imaginings, Murphy's husband, Dennis, was dead, and Isabelle was on
the street, begging to survive. Looking around Isabelle's room, Murphy
knew she was "thinking crazy thoughts," she says, but she couldn't help
herself. Later, she wrote a poem as a way to expel the fear inside of her.
Titling it "Lens," she wrote,

> I see everything through the lens of death.
> I am not dying.
> Perhaps I should be.
> Maybe even wish I were.
> Then I would know.
> I would really know what it is
> that terrifies me so much.

In another poem she wrote while visiting Kabul, Murphy expressed her
horror in learning about the plight of women there. This one she called
"Widow and Child."

> There is no burqa, mother,
> To hide the shame in your eyes,
> No qabali heaped high enough,
> To fill us when father dies.
> You say he was a kind man.
> He did not beat me (often).
> He saved that for the world to do.
> To us in this living coffin,
> There is no burqa, mother,
> That can suffocate my dreams.
> Ah, but for achieving them,
> For that . . . we have no means.

For Murphy, writing poetry freed her from the constraints of objective
reporting, allowing her to express truths that were perhaps too large or
complicated to convey in everyday journalism. Her poems were a chance
for her to process her feelings. In this way, they became a form of self-
care—a critical component of combating psychological stress. In *Emotionally Involved*, Campbell mentions other activities such as yoga, massage,
and "involvement in religious groups/communities of faith" as forms of
self-care. In addition, she notes how support from loved ones can "buffer
many ill effects" of working in the field of trauma. [14]

Several years ago, *St. Paul Pioneer Press* reporter Maja Beckstrom was assigned to write a story about a Minnesota mother of four who'd been murdered by her estranged boyfriend. The man had broken into Latisha Barnes's bedroom and had put a gun to her head while she'd been sleeping. Beckstrom described the scene police encountered after a neighbor's 911 call:

> From the upstairs hall, Officer Wendell saw Latisha's bare legs stretched out on the bedroom carpet. He rushed into the room and found a naked child—Nylah—curled in a fetal position on her mother's bare belly and crying. Nylah wailed more loudly as Officer Spencer snatched her up and felt her icy toes and hands. The first pair of socks she found were an adult's, long enough to cover the toddler's thighs.

Beckstrom, who had a son Nylah's age, couldn't help but imagine him in a similar situation. To cope with all that she was feeling, she often had informal debriefing sessions with her editor, or she simply would enjoy the comfort and stability of her family—her young son and husband. "That helped me regain a sense of equilibrium," says Beckstrom, which allowed her to occasionally delve back into Latisha's violent and tragic world without being overwhelmed by it.

In talking about the consequences of caring, I am not suggesting that journalists' emotions are something of which they should be "cured." After all, journalists have a right to be upset when they witness horrible acts of violence, and as I continue to stress, our emotions can be valuable guides in the reporting process. However, when we are not aware of our emotions—or when they are not in balance with our thoughts—they can wreak havoc on us and cause psychological harm. More important, when we give ourselves the opportunity to process our anger, fear, and grief—perhaps from a more rational and distant perspective—we can begin healing from them. This will be one of the final themes in this book—post-traumatic growth and the American journalist.

NOTES

1. Rebecca Campbell, *Emotionally Involved: The Impact of Researching Rape* (New York: Routledge, 2002), 101–2.

2. Elena Newman, Roger Simpson, and David Handschuh, "Trauma Exposure and Post-Traumatic Stress Disorder Among Photojournalists," *Visual Communications Quarterly* 10, no. 1 (2003): 4–13.

3. Anthony Feinstein, *Dangerous Lives: War and the Men and Women Who Report It* (Toronto: Thomas Allen Publishers, 2003), 24–25, 38, 47, 93, 103.

4. Feinstein, *Dangerous Lives*, 34.

5. Feinstein, *Dangerous Lives*, 101–2.

6. Feinstein, *Dangerous Lives*, 33.

7. Donatella Lorch, "Surviving the Five Ds: A Writer Struggles with the Emotional Aftermath of Covering Brutality in Africa," *Media Studies Journal* (Summer 2001), 98–103.

8. Judith Matloff, "Scathing Memory," *Columbia Journalism Review* (November/December 2004).

9. Matloff, "Scathing Memory."

10. William Prochnau, *Once Upon A Distant War: David Halberstam, Neil Sheehan, Peter Arnett—Young War Correspondents and Their Early Vietnam Battles* (New York: Vintage Books, 1996), 93.

11. Marc Weingarten, *The Gang That Wouldn't Write Straight* (New York: Crown Publishers, 2006), 173–74.

12. Campbell, *Emotionally Involved*, 146, 148.

13. Feinstein, *Dangerous Lives*, 202.

14. Campbell, *Emotionally Involved*, 147–48.

6

❧

Road to Recovery

Finding New Ways to Talk
About—and Heal from—Violence

The last time we talked, Hannah Allam was leaving journalism, at least for the time being. In the summer of 2008, she was about to embark on a one-year fellowship at the Nieman Foundation for Journalism at Harvard University. She recently had become engaged, and she wasn't sure where Baghdad fit into her future. She no longer was the naïve, young reporter who first set foot in Iraq in 2003. The war had changed her, and while her experiences in Iraq had been difficult, she searched for something positive in them, as survivors of trauma often do.

Having prevailed in such trying circumstances, Allam now felt a greater sense of her own personal strength and resilience—gifts she would treasure for the rest of her life. "When I find something really challenging, I'll say to myself, 'I can survive this because I survived [Iraq],'" she told me. "I used to be afraid of flying. Now I think, 'Know what? If it's my day, it's my day.'" A Muslim, Allam had become more connected with her spirituality. "I appreciate the Islamic way of death—three days and then it's frowned upon if you grieve after that, because they [the deceased] are in a better place," she said.

Throughout history, novelists, playwrights, and poets have grappled with the meaning of human suffering. In cultures around the world, myriad protagonists have faced some kind of dragon and, in the end, have emerged from battle stronger than before. More recently, psychiatrists and psychologists have begun to explore a phenomenon known as posttraumatic growth—how suffering can lead to profound, positive changes in a survivor's life. In an article for *Psychiatric Times*, Richard Tedeschi and Lawrence Calhoun, professors of psychology at the University of North

Carolina at Charlotte, describe these changes. They say, "Much like earth-quakes can impact the physical environment, traumatic circumstances, characterized by their unusual, uncontrollable, potentially irreversible and threatening qualities, can produce an upheaval in trauma survivors' major assumptions about the world, their place in it, and how they make sense of their daily lives." These challenges to survivors' assumptions can be the "seeds for new perspectives" on life, say the authors, giving survivors the sense that they have learned valuable lessons and moved forward with their lives.[1]

Reviewing some of the major events of the last decade—September 11, Hurricane Katrina, Virginia Tech, the Iraq War—I wonder whether the American news media haven't undergone a post-traumatic growth process of their own. Can we find hope in our recent struggles? Are we stronger now—more human and more ready to take risks as a result of all that we've endured? And is society ready to consider a new role for us—and to break this country's trauma cycle and view violence as more than a source of entertainment? "What is most energizing about trauma, paradoxically, is that its healing is transformative for the individual as well as for society," says Gina Ross in her book *Beyond the Trauma Vortex*. "Knowing how unresolved trauma engenders pessimism, cynicism, de-spair, and paralysis of the will . . . we can understand how healing opens the door to hope, optimism, and the desire for creative action."[2]

But what is the news media's next step in terms of helping to promote this healing? Where do we go from here with our objective mandate as it pertains to violence and other emotional issues? Obviously, there are no easy solutions here—no "magical leap" forward into the next chapter of journalism. Real change happens in small, sometimes agonizingly incremental steps, like well-traveled terrain that eventually becomes a beaten path. Compared to other forms of the written word, journalism is a relatively new craft. Just a couple of hundred years old, it is still in its in-fancy—still evolving. Like democracy itself, perhaps journalistic objectiv-ity had to run its course—to be played out in its extreme—before we could discover its weaknesses and adapt. After all, only now are we beginning to see how a democratic government can favor those in power—and how an objective news media can give voice to those who already have very loud and influential ones. We still don't know whether there is a better form of government out there, waiting to be discovered, but until we find out, shouldn't we stick with what we have to avoid slipping into some sort of corporate dictatorship? Similarly, if we were to scrap the objective model altogether, how would we keep the news media from descending into opinionated mayhem—or being "bought" by advertisers?

I do not believe the antidote to detached journalism is to stop being reporters—to abandon our search for evidence and our commitment to see as many sides of a story as possible. In advocating for a return to passion in our work, I am not saying that we should set aside our rational, analytic skills in favor of all emotion or all opinion. I don't know if, as journalists, we ever will resolve the tension between objectivity and subjectivity—or if we should try. As I've said, it's in the struggle between the two that we can glean our richest insights. In *Social Science and the Self*, Susan Krieger argues that social science will not collapse with the "more full development of individual and inner perspectives." On the contrary, she says, "[I]ncreased personal understanding can help us think more intelligently and fully about social life." Krieger says her book is about a "wish for something better, for a social science that does not deny the self, but that seeks to use its potential."[3] I have a similar wish for journalists who cover violence—that they will begin to let in their emotions when covering this emotionally difficult topic. After all, there are no "sides" to violence—no reasonable explanations for why people commit it. It's wrong. Period. So why not take a stand against it in our reporting? Why not be outraged when another husband in this country murders his wife, when another child dies at the hands of a parent, when the corpse of another soldier is flown home from Iraq, when another student dies in another school shooting? Why not be sad and grieve for these people—and to allow that sorrow to inform our reporting? The objectivity-at-all-costs model of journalism simply doesn't work when it comes to violence. It's time to create new, more humane—and more realistic—guiding principles.

BEATING A PATH TO CHANGE

In *Emotionally Involved*, Rebecca Campbell often writes about taking a feminist approach to her research. This involves moving beyond the male, objective voice and looking at issues like rape and family violence from the perspective of survivors. This approach encompasses other elements as well, namely collaboration with vested parties and accountability to research subjects. I will explore these two themes in this section as a possible model for journalists who write about violence. In addition, I will look at how a more nuanced approach to teaching journalism and a more diverse newsroom also could encourage a more personally engaged style of reporting.

Collaborative research has a long history in social science, particularly in studies about violence against women. Feminist researchers see tremendous benefit in involving affected parties—advocates and survivors, for instance—in the process of developing goals for research projects and in interpreting the results.[4] According to family violence expert Mary

Gilfus, this approach encourages researchers to see their subjects in a more compassionate, less clinical light:

> A survivor-centered stance involves first and foremost the acknowledgment of the survivor as a complete human being, with a cultural and historical context, capable of expert knowledge, who is a subject in her/his own right, to be viewed through a lens of loving perception. The survivor-centered researcher or practitioner would be prepared to [work] respectfully with expert survivors from various and diverse groups and cultures . . . in order to contribute to a more complex rendering of [violence against women].[5]

Collaborative research also has been referred to as participatory research or survivor-informed research because it values the experiences—the expertise—of those who have survived the violence that is now being studied.

Like so-called parachute journalists, sociologists have been accused of conducting "drive-by" data collection—dropping into a community, collecting what they need, and then dropping out. This can leave a wake of bad feelings among the groups they study. Writing in the international journal *Violence Against Women*, Stephanie Riger, a professor of psychology and gender and women's studies at the University of Illinois, talks about how research subjects in particular may be harmed by this approach. She says:

> This kind of research can be exploitative, benefiting only the researcher and giving nothing back to the community. At its worst, it harms women if the research is designed or interpreted in ways that blame the victim, or is inaccurate, or does not consider the safety and confidentiality of the participants.[6]

As I discussed in chapter 3, similar accusations have been made against journalists who cover violence. When reporters shut themselves off from their emotions and set out to "get" the story at any cost, they risk doing real harm to survivors. In subtle ways, these journalists can end up blaming victims by not putting the abuse in a larger social context. Even worse, when the news media are not accountable to the people about whom they write, they risk further traumatizing crime victims with their aggressive and insensitive tactics.

In social science, collaborative research tears down the hierarchy between researchers and their subjects. As Riger says, "Researchers do not take on the expert role; instead, they acknowledge the value of contributions from all participants." However, these researchers do not abandon their own expertise in the process. "[A]n advocacy stance should not preclude using scientific strategies to minimize bias; criteria of reliability and validity still apply," says Riger.[7]

The idea of a collaborative model of journalism might seem far-fetched. After all, isn't a reporter's job just the opposite—to not get bogged down in other people's agendas? And if journalists are accountable to more than their editors—to the community about which they write and to their subjects—won't they be serving "too many masters"? In fact, collaborative journalism can work, and it has. In 1996, the Rhode Island Coalition Against Domestic Violence (RICADV) launched what they described as a "statewide experiment in participatory communication."[8] Concerned that the state's news media were sensationalizing domestic violence and portraying it as random and inexplicable, RICADV set out to change the tone. They wanted to push domestic violence out of the private realm and have it be seen as a social issue that was "everybody's business."[9]

Adhering to the collaborative approach, RICADV staffers interviewed local print reporters about their overall understanding of domestic violence. Then they created a handbook for the media that responded to what they'd heard. The journalists, in turn, conveyed to the advocates the constraints under which they operated, which helped RICADV develop not only its handbook but its overall communications strategy. For instance, RICADV became much more proactive about calling reporters after a domestic violence incident, and they made themselves readily available to reporters working on deadline.[10]

To assess the effectiveness of these strategies, RICADV hired the Boston College-based Media Research and Action Project (MRAP) to analyze news coverage of domestic violence murders before and after the handbook was disseminated in 2000. To see whether local journalists had adopted any of the best practices RICADV had outlined, MRAP measured, among other things, how often reporters specifically referred to the crimes as domestic violence before and after the creation of the handbook and how often they turned to domestic violence advocates as sources. The study sample included all local print news stories on domestic violence murders occurring four years prior to the handbook (1996—1999, known as Phase 1) and the two years after (2000—2002, known as Phase 2). The results were encouraging.[11]

From Phase 1 to Phase 2, RICADV experienced a significant shift in its influence over the news media's coverage of domestic violence; the agency moved from "media obscurity" and became a go-to source for local reporters covering the crime.[12] More specifically, prior to the publication of the handbook, only half the articles on the murders of intimate partners referred to them as domestic violence, while an astonishing 87 percent of the articles did so in Phase 2. Also in Phase 2, the presence of advocates in these stories doubled, making them the most common lead source.[13] Clearly, the reporters had taken to heart some of the handbook's suggestions.

In a report on their findings, staff from MRAP and RICADV discussed the significance of the shift:

> With broader constituencies framing domestic violence as a social issue, the state's residents and political leaders were readied for the RICADV-led Seven-Point Plan that reformed state policy vis-à-vis domestic violence. The use of domestic violence language by sources other than domestic violence advocates, therefore, suggests a broadened awareness of domestic violence and a culture shift supporting the proposed political change.[14]

In other words, as the state's print media began to portray a more complex picture of domestic violence, advocates began to gain traction elsewhere, leading to significant statewide policy changes.

What is important to note here is that neither party compromised its morals or values in the process of working together. In writing about domestic violence, the state's print reporters did not abandon their mission to gather facts and interview multiple sources. What they did do was deepen their understanding of those facts and put them in context. They also broadened their list of potential sources, moving beyond police and uninformed bystanders like neighbors or co-workers. Likewise, RICADV upheld its mission to end domestic violence in Rhode Island by helping the press—and, thus, the public at large—understand the problem's underlying causes. Each party gained greater insight into the other's needs and perspective, which ultimately made them better at their jobs.

In discussing the concept of letting in our emotions and personal experiences as reporters, I would be remiss if I also did not mention the need for more diversity in the newsroom. This would allow our audiences to see a more "balanced" view of the world from multiple perspectives. Hannah Allam, for instance, had a very different reaction to the Iraq War than some of her colleagues. A Muslim who'd spent part of her childhood in the Middle East, she felt personally connected to the people about whom she wrote. As a result, her reports from the frontlines were filled with emotion, and Allam didn't shy away from using graphic details as a way to convey the depth of the tragedies she'd witnessed. "After one bombing, a young boy shoved a severed hand in my face," she wrote in one report from 2004. "Another time, I used a tissue to pick shreds of human flesh off my shoes after covering a car bombing. Gagging, I gave up and pushed the sneakers deep into the trash."[15]

Perspectives like Allam's are critical if we are to move beyond the which-side-is-winning type of war reporting to something more profound. In breaching the barrier between "us and them," Allam embraced her own voice rather than the objective, white male voice, which, sadly, still dominates most newsrooms. According to the American Society of Newspaper Editors, only 13.5 of America's daily print reporters and only

11.4 percent of all newsroom supervisors are minorities.[16] Clearly, this is not an adequate reflection of the population as a whole, especially when it comes to violence. In the U.S., minorities make up about 34 percent of the population, and they are much more likely to be victims of a crime than non-minorities. In 2005, for instance, the homicide rate for African Americans was *six* times higher than the rate for whites.[17]

In addition, women working full-time at daily newspapers now total 19,700—or roughly 37 percent—which means they are still underrepresented among the U.S. news media as well.[18] As I stated in chapter 4, female journalists can play a vital role in allowing emotions to enter the newsroom dialogue. Because women tend to be more comfortable sharing their feelings, these reporters can make it safer for male colleagues to be emotional as well.

In addition to race and gender, newsrooms need to do a better job in recruiting reporters from different socioeconomic backgrounds. In his CJR article on rethinking objectivity, Brent Cunningham says that a "bias born of class" is one of the news media's most damaging biases of all. He contends that because newsrooms tend to focus their diversity efforts on race, gender, and ethnicity, they attract journalists "with different skin color but largely the same middle-class background and aspirations."[19] This can lead to what National Public Radio's Jonathan Kern describes as an "echo chamber" in the newsroom. In this scenario, "reporters and editors fail to represent some viewpoints mainly because they all see events from the same perspective."[20] For example, middle-class, college-educated journalists might view poverty very differently from someone who has actually lived through it.

My final thought on encouraging a more emotionally engaged style of journalism is to have more seasoned practitioners teaching journalism in college—men and women who have lived and breathed violence and trauma and understand how difficult (and perhaps even undesirable) an objective approach to these emotional issues can be. This would start the process of destigmatizing emotions early and would help dismantle the "culture of silence" that has become the journalistic norm. Unfortunately, as schools compete to be among the top 100 in *U.S. News & World Report*'s annual rankings, more colleges and universities seem to be bypassing experienced journalists in favor of those with prestige-boosting PhDs. According to one survey, 17 percent of journalism educators have never worked as journalists, and 47 percent have less then ten years experience as journalists.[21]

Jim Willis, chair of the Department of Communication Studies at Azusa Pacific University in Southern California, fears this trend will continue to result in student journalists learning about objectivity and emotions in overly simplistic ways. "Emotional aspects of reporting are controversial among even veteran reporters; they are not really understood by those who haven't practiced journalism much firsthand, and many of those are found teaching journalism in the classroom," he says. With nothing else on which to rely, these inexperienced instructors "punt and go with the textbook notion of total detachment, neutral verbiage," he says, and their students end up graduating from these programs unprepared for the emotional challenges they will face. The result, says Willis, is a "degree of sterility" perpetuated in their coverage.

In the journalism classes I teach, I will err on the side of feelings and opinions rather than neutrality to discourage this type of emotional sterility. In one exercise, students work to define the nut paragraphs of their stories; I ask them to tell me how they feel about their topics. I tell them to write down their opinions (e.g., the lack of affordable health care in the United States is wrong, or colleges are violating students' rights with overly intrusive speech codes). In this very basic seed of emotion—compassion, anger, despair—we find the essence of their stories. If they feel outrage, I encourage them to explore the reasons why, to let that emotion be their guide. Oftentimes, it is the only way I can get them to articulate a thesis for their articles—that every U.S. citizen has a right to quality medical care, for instance, or that colleges should encourage the free exchange of ideas rather than repress them for their own purposes.

In another exercise I do—usually on the first day of class as a way of introducing myself—I ask the students to pretend that they are interviewing me for a profile in their college newspaper. At first, they ask the typically polite questions—where are you from, why did you decide to get into teaching, what was your favorite assignment as a journalist, and so forth. After this, I tell them to think of another question—something that they thought about asking me the first time, but were perhaps too afraid or embarrassed to do so. Usually, these questions come from a deeper place in them, stemming from curiosity rather than formality: Were you ever afraid when traveling abroad on assignment? Are you married? Did you ever feel like giving up on your dream of becoming a journalist? Of course, these are the questions that make for a compelling profile, and the students learn from this exercise that they are their greatest resource when it comes to reporting—that their curiosity, which often stems from their own personal experiences, will lead to the richest material.

This exercise also forces me as an instructor to come out from behind my professional facade and reveal myself to my students. In order to get them to express their emotions, I first must "normalize" my own, which means answering their questions as honestly as possible, even if it makes me uncomfortable. In this way, the first person slowly begins to enter our dialogue—the elephant in the room is on its way to being seen. In tapping into their inner worlds, the students start to make sense of their outer worlds as would-be journalists.

These small steps that I have proposed here—more collaborative types of projects, more diversity in the newsroom, more practitioners in the classroom, and a more nuanced approach to teaching young reporters— are only the start of what I hope will be a larger discussion on the value of emotions in journalism. Many journalistic trends have come and gone (e.g., New Journalism and even, to some extent, Citizen Journalism), but our dissatisfaction with the objective mandate persists. It may take us a while to figure out what to do with this—how to keep what's right with journalism and how to shed those parts that hold us back from connecting with our stories in more meaningful ways. But I do believe that, one reporter at a time, we are moving in that direction.

HOPE

As a family sociologist and feminist, Kersti Yllo often has thought of herself as a bridge between the different approaches to researching family violence. She tells me that while most sociologists still study the issue from an "objectivist" position, more qualitative work is starting to emerge. "The schism has really abated," she says, "and one of the things I've tried over the years is to be a translator between hard-core researchers and activists." She recalls the first international conference on family violence in the early 1980s at the University of New Hampshire. Activists were angry about the researchers' detached and clinical approach to what they, the activists, saw as a dire problem. "The activists were shouting down the researchers, who were shocked," says Yllo. "But then we listened to each other for a while, and we got older." Today, she contends, both parties are beginning to see the merits of the other's approach—and how they can work together to create a more complete picture of family violence.

In a similar way, I see many of the reporters profiled in this book as translators between two worlds—the objective and the subjective in journalism. Journalists like Hannah Allam, Miles Moffeit, and Daniel Vargas are subtly changing the newsroom culture by tuning into their emotions—and daring to talk about them. Allam, for instance, has not shied away from publicly discussing her struggles with post-traumatic stress, including at a forum sponsored by the Dart Center. As a result, she has had several journalists approach her for help in dealing with their own job-related stress. "I've passed out my former Cairo therapist's number to *six* of my friends returning from Iraq," she says. David Handschuh, the *New York Daily News* photographer who nearly lost his life on September 11, compares this gradual process of change to the old Faberge shampoo commercials in which "You tell two friends and then they tell two friends and so on and so on." Through one-on-one conversations, emotionally engaged reporting is gaining a presence in the newsroom.

On a broader scale, the American news media are more seriously considering the emotional impact certain stories may have on their audiences. As an example, Dart's Bruce Shapiro mentions the major news media's coverage of Virginia Tech. After a backlash from their audiences and some of the victims' families, the networks decided to pull back on airing Seung-Hui Cho's disturbing video manifesto in which he poses with a gun. According to Shapiro, ABC News even consulted with a mental health expert about the danger of audiences seeing the video over and over again, and the network decided to stop airing the manifesto after the first twenty-four hours.

Shapiro says he agreed with the networks' initial decision to show the video because it "allowed people to draw their own conclusions and to see the truth." Rather than becoming embroiled in a national debate about the declining moral values of teenagers, the news media showed Virginia Tech for what it was—the twisted act of "one very sick kid," he says. At least for these media outlets, then, the Virginia Tech story was not a case of "all or nothing." The networks did not hide behind the banner of objectivity, continue to show the video, and assume no responsibility for its impact on their audiences. But neither did they completely crumble in the face of criticism and withhold vital information. "There was some responsible decision-making informed by a greater emotional awareness," says Shapiro.

Of course, any time the news media step away from the journalistic model of detachment, they are more vulnerable to criticism. But they also are more likely to grow as professionals—and people. In no longer seeing themselves as "other," journalists who cover violence are more open to the lessons their subjects have to teach them, often about courage and resilience. When Vargas finished his series about Angela Hudson, the woman burned alive by her estranged husband, he experienced a kind of survivor's guilt that motivated him to make changes in his own life. "You start to think, 'I'm lucky to be in the situation that I'm in. Now what am I going to do with it?'" he tells me. Two and a half years after the series was published, Vargas quit his job at the paper to pursue his lifelong dream of writing a book. He is certain that if he had not met Hudson, he would not have had the courage to do so.

In *Emotionally Involved*, Campbell says that she and her research team also grew from their experiences interviewing rape survivors. At times, the process was incredibly painful for them, but because the researchers allowed themselves to connect with the survivors on a more intimate level, they gained strength from the women's stories. Campbell describes the feelings this instilled in her and her team. She says:

It's hard to get an exact label for this—it's certainly not "happiness," "joy," or "gladness." It's about connecting with other women, feeling pride in their strength and in our collective strength, helping someone in ways you didn't expect, feeling part of someone's life. Having those experiences nurtures hope—for the survivor, for yourself, for women, for a future free from violence.[22]

The reporters I spoke with described a similar experience. In talking and writing about violence in a different way, they felt that they were helping to lift some of the stigma around it. In addition, the relationships they formed with their subjects buoyed them during personally difficult moments. Of course, throwing off the yoke of objectivity is complicated. It means coming out from behind our masks as "impartial outsiders" and emerging as vulnerable human beings. Still, none of the reporters I interviewed had any regrets. In the space between the subjective and the objective, they had found their stories' truths—and their own.

NOTES

1. Richard G. Tedeschi and Lawrence Calhoun, "Posttraumatic Growth: A New Perspective on Psychotraumatology," *Psychiatric Times* 21, no. 4, April 1 2004. www.psychiatrictimes.com/display/article/10168/54661 (accessed August 3, 2008).

2. Gina Ross, *Beyond the Trauma Vortex: The Media's Role in Healing Fear, Terror, and Violence* (Berkeley, Calif.: North Atlantic Books, 2003), 110–11.

3. Susan Krieger, *Social Science and the Self: Personal Essays on an Art Form* (New Brunswick, N.J.: Rutgers University Press, 1991), 1–2.

4. Stephanie Riger, "Guest Editor's Introduction: Working Together: Challenges in Collaborative Research on Violence Against Women," *Violence Against Women* 5, no. 10 (1999): 1099–1117.

5. Mary E. Gilfus et al., "Research on Violence Against Women: Creating Survivor-Informed Collaborations," *Violence Against Women* 5, no. 10 (1999): 1194–1212.

6. Riger, "Guest Editor's Introduction," 1101.

7. Riger, "Guest Editor's Introduction," 1109, 1111.

8. Charlotte Ryan et al., "Changing Coverage of Domestic Violence: A Longitudinal Experiment in Participatory Communication," *Journal of Interpersonal Violence* 21, no. 2 (2006): 209–28.

9. Charlotte Ryan et al., "Start Small, Build Big: Negotiating Opportunities in Media Markets," *Mobilization: An International Journal* 10, no. 1 (2005): 101–17.

10. Ryan et al., "Changing Coverage of Domestic Violence," 223.

11. Ryan et al., "Changing Coverage of Domestic Violence," 216.

12. Ryan et al., "Start Small, Build Big," 101.

13. Ryan et al., "Changing Coverage of Domestic Violence," 218.

14. Ryan et al., "Start Small, Build Big," 115.

15. Hannah Allam, "Increasing Dangers in Iraq Make Reporting the Whole Truth Tough," Knight Ridder Washington Bureau, November 19, 2004.

16. American Society of Newspaper Editors, *Newsrooms Shrink; Minority Percentages Increase Slightly*, 2008. www.asne.org/files/08Census.pdf (accessed July 3, 2008).

17. U.S. Department of Justice, Bureau of Justice Statistics, *Homicide Trends in the U.S.*, 2005, www.ojp.usdoj.gov/bjs/homicide/race.htm (accessed July 3, 2008).

18. American Society of Newspaper Editors, *Newsrooms Shrink; Minority Percentages Increase Slightly*.

19. Brent Cunningham, "Toward a New Ideal: Re-thinking Objectivity in a World of Spin," *Columbia Journalism Review* (July/August 2003).

20. Jonathan Kern, *Sound Reporting: The NPR Guide to Audio Journalism and Production* (Chicago: University of Chicago Press, 2008), 11.

21. Betty Medsger, *Winds of Change: Challenges Confronting Journalism Education*, The Freedom Forum, Arlington, Va., 1996.

22. Rebecca Campbell, *Emotionally Involved: The Impact of Researching Rape* (New York: Routledge, 2002), 90.

Bibliography

Agee, James. *Let Us Now Praise Famous Men*. Boston: Houghton Mifflin, 1941.

Alan, Jeff. Interview with A.J. Hammer, *Showbiz Tonight*, CNN, September 12, 2005.

Allam, Hannah. "Increasing Dangers in Iraq Make Reporting the Whole Truth Tough." Knight Ridder Washington Bureau, November 19, 2004.

Alterman Eric. "'Objectivity RIP.'" *Nation*, December 24, 2001.

———. "Out of Print: The Death and Life of the American Newspaper." *New Yorker*, March 31, 2008.

Alvis-Banks, Donna. "When Hometown News Becomes Worldwide News." *Traumatology* 14, no. 1 (March 2008): 85–88.

American Society of Newspaper Editors. *Newsrooms Shrink; Minority Percentages Increase Slightly*. 2008. www.asne.org/files/08Census.pdf.

Anderson, Scott. "The Lives They Lived; The Target." *New York Times*, December 29, 2002, Magazine.

Berns, Nancy. *Framing the Victim: Domestic Violence, Media and Social Problems*. New York: Aldine de Gruyter, 2004.

Berry, Stephen J. "Why Objectivity Still Matters." *Nieman Reports* 59.2 (Summer 2005).

Bliss, Edward Jr., ed. *In Search of the Light: The Broadcasts of Edward R. Murrow 1938–1961*. New York: Alfred A. Knopf, 1967.

Boyer, Peter J. "One Angry Man." *New Yorker*, June 23, 2008.

Campbell, Rebecca. *Emotionally Involved: The Impact of Researching Rape*. New York: Routledge, 2002.

Carey, James W. "Why and How? The Dark Continent of American Journalism." Pp. 146–96 in *Reading the News: A Pantheon Guide to Popular Culture*, edited by Robert Karl Manoff and Michael Schudson. New York: Pantheon Books, 1996.

Colbert, Stephen. *The Colbert Report*, Comedy Central, October 17, 2005.

Cooper, Anderson. *Dispatches from the Edge: A Memoir of War, Disasters, and Survival*. New York: HarperCollins, 2006.

Edwards, Bob. *Edward R. Murrow and the Birth of Broadcast Journalism.* Hoboken, N.J.: John Wiley & Sons, 2004.

Feinstein, Anthony. *Dangerous Lives: War and the Men and Women Who Report It.* Toronto: Thomas Allen Publishers, 2003.

Ferrand Bullock, Cathy and Jason Cubert. "Coverage of Domestic Violence Fatalities by Newspapers in Washington State." *Journal of Interpersonal Violence* 17, no. 5 (May 2002): 475–99.

Franiuk, Renae et al. "Prevalence and Effects of Rape Myths in Print Journalism." *Violence Against Women* 14, no. 3 (March 2008): 287–309.

Gilfus, Mary E. "The Price of the Ticket: A Survivor-Centered Appraisal of Trauma Theory." *Violence Against Women* 5, no. 11 (November 1999): 1238–1257.

Gilfus, Mary E. et al. "Research on Violence Against Women: Creating Survivor-Informed Collaborations." *Violence Against Women* 5, no. 10 (October 1999): 1194–1212.

Goleman, Daniel. *Emotional Intelligence: Why It Can Matter More than IQ.* New York: Bantam Books, 1995.

Greene, Joshua D. et al. "The Neural Bases of Cognitive Conflict and Control in Moral Judgment." *Neuron* 44 (October 14, 2004): 389–400.

Handschuh, David. "A Lens on Life and Death." PoynterOnline 2002. www.poynter.org/content/content_view.asp?id=4673.

Herr, Michael. *Dispatches.* New York: Vintage Books, 1991.

Hight, Joe and Frank Smyth. *Tragedies & Journalists: A Guide for More Effective Coverage.* Dart Center for Journalism and Trauma (2003).

Humphries, Drew, ed. *Women, Violence, and the Media: Readings in Feminist Criminology.* Boston: Northeastern University Press, 2009.

Inglis, Fred. *People's Witness: The Journalist in Modern Politics.* New Haven, Conn: Yale University Press, 2002.

Kakutani, Michiko. "Mailer Talking." *New York Times,* June 6, 1982.

Kazin, Alfred. "The Trouble He's Seen: *The Armies of the Night* by Norman Mailer." *New York Times,* 5 May 1968.

Kern, Jonathan. *Sound Reporting: The NPR Guide to Audio Journalism and Production.* Chicago: University of Chicago Press, 2008.

Kleinman, Sherryl. "Feminist Fieldwork Analysis." *Qualitative Research Methods Series* 51. Thousand Oaks, Calif.: Sage Publications, Inc., 2007.

Krieger, Susan. *Social Science and the Self: Personal Essays on an Art Form.* New Brunswick, N.J.: Rutgers University Press, 1991.

Landrieu, Mary. Interview with George Stephanopoulos, *This Week with George Stephanopoulos,* ABC News, 4 September 2005.

Lorch, Donatella. "Surviving the Five Ds: A Writer Struggles with the Emotional Aftermath of Covering Brutality in Africa." *Media Studies Journal* (Summer 2001): 98–103.

Lung, Ching-Tun and Deborah Daro. "Current Trends in Child Abuse Reporting and Fatalities: The Results of the 1995 Annual Fifty State Survey." Chicago: National Committee to Prevent Child Abuse (1996).

Mabaridge, Dale. "Close Enough to Hurt." *Columbia Journalism Review.* January/February 2005.

Mailer, Norman. *The Armies of the Night: History As a Novel, The Novel as History.* New York: Plume, 1994.

Matloff, Judith. "Scathing Memory." *Columbia Journalism Review,* November/December 2004.

Medsger, Betty. *Winds of Change: Challenges Confronting Journalism Education*. The Freedom Forum, Arlington, Va. (1996).

Melton, Gary B. "Chronic Neglect of Family Violence: More Than a Decade of Reports to Guide U.S. Policy." *Child Abuse & Neglect* 26, Issues 6–7 (June 2002): 569–86.

Meyers, Marian. *News Coverage of Domestic Violence: Engendering Blame*. Thousand Oaks, Calif.: Sage Publications, Inc., 1997.

Mindich, David T. Z. *Just the Facts: How Objectivity Came to Define American Journalism*. New York: New York University Press, 1998.

Newman, Elena et al. "Trauma Exposure and Post-Traumatic Stress Disorder Among Photojournalists." *Visual Communications Quarterly* 10, no. 1 (2003): 4–13.

Ochberg, Frank. "Trauma News: Story in Three Acts." Gift From Within. www.giftfromwithin.org/html/threeact.html.

———. "There Is Reason in Action." Pp. 135–49 in *Mapping Trauma and Its Wake: Autobiographic Essays by Pioneer Trauma Scholars* (Routledge Psychosocial Stress Series, 31), edited by Charles R. Figley. New York: Routledge, 2005.

Office of Georgia Rep. John Lewis. *Rep. John Lewis on Death of Journalist David Halberstam*. State News Service, April 23, 2007.

Paine, Thomas. *Common Sense*. American Revolution Primary Sources. UXL-GALE, 2005. eNotes.com, 2006. www.enotes.com/american-revolution-primary-sources/thomas-paine-common-sense.

Pedelty, Mark. *War Stories: The Culture of Foreign Correspondents*. New York: Routledge, 1995.

The Pew Research Center for People & the Press. *Public More Critical of Press, but Goodwill Persists*. 2005 people-press.org/report/248/public-more-critical-of-press-but-goodwill-persists.

Pinkerton, Jim. Interview with Eric Burns, *Fox News Watch*, Fox News Network, September 10, 2005.

Prochnau, William. *Once Upon a Distant War: David Halberstam, Neil Sheehan, Peter Arnett—Young War Correspondents and Their Early Vietnam Battles*. New York: Vintage Books, 1996.

———. "The Upside of Anger: A David Halberstam Appreciation." *American Journalism Review*, June/July 2007.

Project for Excellence in Journalism. *State of the News Media 2007: An Annual Report on American Journalism*. 2007. Washington, D.C.: Project for Excellence in Journalism.

Rand, Michael and Shannon Catalano. "Criminal Victimization, 2006." *Bureau of Justice Statistics Bulletin* (December 2007).

Rather, Dan. Interview with David Letterman, *Late Show with David Letterman*, CBS, 17 September 2001.

Richardson, Sherry. "Confronting the Horror." *American Journalism Review*, January/February 1999.

Riger, Stephanie. "Guest Editor's Introduction: Working Together: Challenges in Collaborative Research on Violence Against Women," *Violence Against Women* 5, no. 10 (October 1999): 1099–1117.

Rosen, Jay. *What Are Journalists For?* New Haven, Conn.: Yale University Press, 1999.

Ross, Gina. *Beyond the Trauma Vortex: The Media's Role in Healing Fear, Terror, and Violence*. Berkeley, Calif.: North Atlantic Books, 2003.

Rubin, Harriet. "TV: Why a Little 'Dry' Journalism Would Serve Us All." *USA Today*, 29 September 2005.

Ryan, Charlotte et al. "Start Small, Build Big: Negotiating Opportunities in Media Markets." *Mobilization: An International Journal* 10, no. 1 (2005): 101–17.

Ryan, Charlotte et al. "Changing Coverage of Domestic Violence: A Longitudinal Experiment in Participatory Communication." *Journal of Interpersonal Violence* 21, no. 2 (February 2006): 209–228.

Schudson, Michael. *Discovering the News: A Sociological History of American Newspapers*. New York: Basic Books, Inc., 1978.

———. *The Power of News*. Cambridge, Mass.: Harvard University Press, 1995.

———. *The Sociology of News*. New York: W.W. Norton & Company, Inc., 2003.

Schudson, Michael and Danielle Haas. "One of the Guys." *Columbia Journalism Review*, March/April 2008.

Scott Collins, Karen et al. "Health Concerns Across a Woman's Lifespan: The Commonwealth Fund 1998 Survey of Women's Health." The Commonwealth Fund (May 1999).

Shapiro, Bruce. "One Violent Crime." *Nation*, April 3, 1995.

Sheehan, Neil. *A Bright Shining Lie: John Paul Vann and America in Vietnam*. New York: Vintage Books, 1989.

Smith, Allen C. III and Sherryl Kleinman. "Managing Emotions in Medical School: Students' Contacts with the Living and the Dead." *Social Psychology Quarterly* 52, no. 1, Special Issue: Sentiments, Affect and Emotion (March 1989): 56–69.

Tedeschi, Richard G. and Lawrence Calhoun. "Posttraumatic Growth: A New Perspective on Psychotraumatology." *Psychiatric Times* 21, no. 4, April 1, 2004, www.psychiatrictimes.com/display/article/10168/54661.

U.S. Department of Justice/Bureau of Justice Statistics. *Homicide Trends in the U.S.* 2005. www.ojp.usdoj.gov/bjs/homicide/race.htm.

Vargas, Daniel. "Legacy of Love & Pain." *Houston Chronicle*, 24 February 2002.

———. *Acceptance Speech*. Given at the Dart Center for Journalism & Trauma's annual Dart Award for Excellence in Reporting on Victims of Violence ceremony, McGraw-Hill Auditorium, New York, April 2003.

Vogt, Andrea. "Memories of the '60s Still Hearten Writer; Journalist David Halberstam Speaks on Civil Rights Movement." *Spokesman Review*, April 9, 1999.

Weingarten, Marc. *The Gang That Wouldn't Write Straight: Wolfe, Thompson, Didion, and the New Journalism Revolution*. New York: Crown Publishers, 2006.

Willis, Jim. *The Human Journalist: Reporters, Perspectives, and Emotions*. Westport, Conn.: Praeger Publishers, 2003.

Wolfe, Tom. *The New Journalism*. London: Picador, 1975.

Yllo, Kersti. "Political and Methodological Debates in Wife Abuse Research." Pp. 28–50 in *Feminist Perspectives on Wife Abuse*, edited by Kersti Yllo and Michele Bograd. Newbury Park, Calif.: Sage Publications, Inc., 1988.

Index

Agee, James, 15–16, 44
Allam, Hannah: conflict press corps as a "men's club," 61; dealing with emotional stress, 67; experiences as an Arab American in Iraq, 49, 76; isolation of war reporters, 64; leaving journalism, 71; murder of translator's family, 59; post-traumatic stress of, 60, 79; pressure to suppress emotions, 49–50

Beckstrom, Maja, 69
Berns, Nancy, 5–6, 7–8
Brokaw, Tom, 28
Bryant, Kobe. *See* coverage of interpersonal violence
Burke, Kevin, 53

Calhoun, Lawrence, 71–72
Campbell, Rebecca: achieving "emotional peace," xxiv; caring for ourselves, 66–67, 68; caring for research participants, 37; defining rape, xiii; emotional growth of, 80–81; emotional impact of interviewing rape survivors, 60; emotion work theory, 43–44; feminist approach to research, 73; importance of emotions in social sciences, xiii–xiv; interviewing research subjects, 54; lack of emotion in rape research, 34; rape culture, 48; "researching the researcher," xxiv

Carey, James, 5
Carr, Tina, 56, 57
Cho, Seung-Hui. *See* Virginia Tech
Colbert, Stephen, 27
collaborative research, 73–76
Cooper, Anderson, xvii, xix, xxi, 35
coverage of interpersonal violence: blaming the victim, 3–4; Bryant, Kobe, 8–9; emotion as the main element of, 34–35; feminist analysis of, 4; media bias in crimes covered, 6–7; news media's failure to give a social context for, 5–6; Peterson, Laci, 7; police and other officials as biased sources, 5. *See also* Meyers, Marian
Cunningham, Brent, 9, 28, 77

Dart Center for Journalism & Trauma, 37, 38, 39, 67. *See also* Ochberg, Frank; Shapiro, Bruce

diversity in newsrooms (or lack of),
76–77

emotionally engaged reporting:
being more sensitive to victims
of violence, 37–38; benefits to
journalists, 41–42; bloggers as
emotional journalists, 27; capturing
a more complex truth, 44; finding
a middle ground with objectivity,
28; fine line between feeling
emotions and being ruled by them,
43–44; forming more intimate
relationships with subjects, 35–36;
helping audiences break cycle of
violence, 39–41; historic roots of,
16–18; irrational passion of political
pundits, 26–27, 28; second "big
bang" of journalism, 28–29. *See also*
Vietnam War

Feinstein, Anthony, 50, 56–57, 63–66.
See also psychological impact of
covering war
Franiuk, Renae, 8–9
freelancers. *See* Carr, Tina; Feinstein,
Anthony; psychological stress of
covering war

Gellhorn, Martha. *See* World War II
gender: childbirth contributing to
psychological stress of female
war reporters, 50; macho culture
of newsroom, 61; male reporters
covering sexual assault, 51;
objective voice in journalism as
white male voice, 49; women
assigned to more emotional topics,
48; women journalists not allowed
to be as openly emotional as men,
48, 49; women leading the way
in more emotionally engaged
reporting, 51–52. *See also* Allam,
Hannah; Lundeen, Bruce; Murphy,
Beth; Sullivan, Laura
Gilfus, Mary E., 73–74
Goleman, Daniel, xiii, xx

Greene, Joshua, xiii

Halberstam, David, 21–22, 23. *See also*
Vietnam War
Handschuh, David, xviii–xx, 79–80
Herr, Michael, xvi–xvii, 66. *See also*
Vietnam War
Hudson, Angela. *See* Vargas, Daniel
Hurricane Katrina, xvii, xix, xx, 67. *See
also* Cooper, Anderson

Inglis, Fred, 17, 20

journalism education, xvii, 2, 77–79

Kern, Jonathan, 77
Kleinman, Sherryl, 11
Krieger, Susan, 2, 36, 73

Lombardi, Kristen, 61
Lorch, Donnatella, 65
Lundeen, Bruce, 51–52, 53

Mailer, Norman, 25–26. *See also*
Vietnam War
Matloff, Judith, 53, 65
Media Research and Action Project,
75–76
Meloy, Michelle L., 6–7
Meyers, Marian, 4–7
Miller, Susan L., 6–7
Mindich, David T. Z., 18, 28–29
Moffeit, Miles, xv, xxi, 35, 36, 51
Moniz, Frank, xi–xii, xxi
Moniz, Maryellen, xi–xii, xxi
Murphy, Beth: becoming numb to
images of violence, 54; becoming
pregnant, 50; capturing emotional
complexities, 52; connecting with
female documentary subjects, 47–48;
controlling her emotions, 44; dealing
with emotional stress, 68; gender as a
liability in journalism, 49; poems, 68
Murrow, Edward R., 19–21, 35

New Journalism. *See* Mailer, Norman;
Wolfe, Thomas; Vietnam War

objectivity: having a negative impact on the news, xviii; history of, 18–19; journalistic tradition of, xvii–xviii, 2–3; modeled after "scientific knowing," 1; rituals of, 1–2. *See also* coverage of interpersonal violence; Schudson, Michael

Ochberg, Frank: awareness of (versus preoccupation with) emotions, 10; overcoming our violent heritage, xvi; paradoxical pleasure of violence, xv–xvi; post-traumatic stress, 62–63, 64, 66; response of other "first responders" to stress of violence, 61–62; reversing human tendency to respond to suffering with cruelty, 39; three acts of violence, 40–41

Oklahoma City bombing, 1, 34. *See also* Willis, Jim

Olbermann, Keith, 26–28

O'Reilly, Bill, xviii, 26–28

participatory research. *See* collaborative research

Pearl, Daniel, 63

Pedelty, Mark, 57

Peterson, Laci. *See* coverage of domestic violence

Plato, xii

post-traumatic growth, 71–72

post-traumatic stress disorder (PTSD). *See* psychological impact of covering violence

Prochnau, William, 21–22, 65–66

psychological impact of covering violence: childbirth as an aggravating factor, 50; freelancers, 56–57; hesitancy to admit to emotional problems, 61; news media lagging in providing counseling, 61–62; news organizations' response to, 61–62, 67; post-traumatic stress disorder (PTSD), 62–63, 64–66; self-care, 66–69; videographers suffering

more, 52–53; war reporters, 63–66. *See also* Allam, Hannah; Feinstein, Anthony; Matloff, Judith; Ochberg, Frank

public distrust of news media, 9

Pyle, Ernie. *See* World War II

Rather, Dan, xx, 28–29

Rhode Island Coalition Against Domestic Violence, 75–76

Riger, Stephanie, 74

Rory Peck Trust, 56, 57

Rosen, Jay, 10

Ross, Gina, 39–40, 72

Schudson, Michael: empathy as key to good journalism, 52; evolution of objectivity, 17, 18–19, 20–21; power of the news media in shaping public policy, 8; Vietnam era, 23

September 11, xix–xx, 47. *See also* Handschuh, David

Shapiro, Bruce, xix, 38–39, 80

Sheehan, Neil, 21, 23

subjectivity: emotions as evidence, 11; finding a balance with objectivity, 72–73; mediating between inner and outer worlds, 1012; thinking versus feeling, xii–xiii

Sullivan, Andrew, 27

Sullivan, Laura, 37–38, 50–51, 53–55

Tedeschi, Richard, 71–72

Vargas, Daniel: emotional growth of, 80; personal experience with violence, 33–34, 51; psychological stress of, 60–61; refusing to blame a victim of violence, 4; series on Angela Hudson, 33–34

Vietnam War: end of war, 25; inspiring a new kind of journalism, 16, 21, 23; New Journalism, 23–26; psychic toll on journalists, 66; resulting in a culture of criticism, 23. *See also* Halberstam, David; Herr, Jonathan; Mailer, Norman

Virginia Tech, xiv, xx–xxi, 80
visual journalists, 48, 52–53. *See also* Handschuh, David; Lundeen, Bruce; Matloff, Judith

war reporters. *See* psychological impact of covering violence
Weingarten, Marc, 24, 25, 66

Willis, Jim, 1, 34–35, 77–78
Wolfe, Thomas, 23, 24, 28, 37
World War II: Gellhorn, Martha, 17, 19; journalists taking a stand in their reporting, 19; Pyle, Ernie, 19, 65–66. *See also* Murrow, Edward R.

Yllo, Kersti, 10, 11, 48, 49, 79

About the Author

Jody Santos is an award-winning journalist and documentary filmmaker. She has reported for television and print news for the last twenty years, and has been producing and directing documentaries for PBS and cable networks like Discovery Health and the Hallmark Channel since 2000. She has traveled to more than a dozen countries across five continents, documenting everything from the trafficking of girls in Nepal to the reproductive rights of women in Ghana.

Regardless of the medium, her goal has remained the same: to shed light on the social injustices of the day. Her reports often focus on the issue of violence against women and children and ways to prevent violence in our communities. As a special projects producer for Boston's NBC news affiliate, she was nominated for an Emmy for a special report on an effort to rid the city's streets of black market guns. In 2003, she won a Telly for a public television documentary on the rights of women in third world countries.

Over the years, Santos has appeared on National Public Radio, *Unsolved Mysteries*, and other news outlets to defend her writings and weigh in on important current events. She is assistant professor of communications at Springfield College.